EMBRACING
the POWER *of*
AI

EMBRACING
the POWER *of*
AI

A Gentle CXO Guide

Roundtree Press

CONTENTS

EMBRACING *the* POWER *of* AI - 29

PART I
THE NEW FRONTIER - 30
OVERVIEW - 33

PART IV

TOOLS - 100
OVERVIEW - 103

PART V

AI AT WORK - 126
OVERVIEW - 129

PREFACE

From the Authors

Artificial intelligence (AI) is a game-changer for the way in which companies work and interact with customers. Some visionaries posit that AI will become as basic as electricity. It will inevitably shake up the status quo with regard to the way companies operate and how they build their software.

Being a pure-play digital company, specializing in innovative technologies, Globant foresees that every single product we build will leverage AI, and we are all exploring that potential.

The aim of this book is to enable you to feel comfortable with the principles of AI, so that you don't feel lost and don't miss opportunities. The point is not to build an army of AI specialists, but rather to build an AI-capable culture. Whether this book is a refresher, a starting point, or an immersive experience in the world of AI, the goal is to provide you with enough information to give you an intuitive sense of this emerging technology so that you can be part of any team and initiative that embraces it.

FOREWORD

The AI Factor: The Power of Ubiquitous Intelligence

In **the opening scene** of the seminal 1982 film *Blade Runner*, an interrogator asks an android named Leon questions "designed to provoke an emotional response." Because, in the movie's dystopian future, empathy is the one feature that distinguishes humans from artificial intelligence (AI). Leon knows this as well, so when the interrogator begins asking questions about his mother, he stands up, pulls out his gun, and abruptly ends the interview.

Pop culture references to AI like this one have for decades depicted man pitted against machine. And they continue to do so, because the more we know about AI, the more we appreciate how fundamentally it will alter human society.

We've experienced similarly powerful explosions of technology in the recent past. Over the past ten years, customers and consumers were told many technologies would fundamentally change their lives, including big data, 3D printing, digital wallets, IOT, wearable devices, augmented and virtual reality. Regardless of this, none of them—except maybe for the smartphone—provoked a reaction as dramatic as the current hair-pulling and chest-beating over AI.

If we think clearly, we realize that AI offers powerful value propositions to enhance human capabilities. We can easily envision AI algorithms that increase human intelligence in different dimensions, especially areas where humans trail in competency. Kevin Kelly made this very point in an article he wrote for *Wired*, saying, "Intelligence is not a single dimension, so 'smarter than humans' is a meaningless concept. And humans do not have general purpose minds, and neither will AIs."[1]

Each intelligence dimension presents a new opportunity for an AI application to enhance and propel its potential. Therefore, while many pundits proclaim AI will replace humans, we see AI synergizing with existing technology and humans, opening up amazing new paths along the road. Therefore, rather than talk about Artificial Intelligence, we like to talk about augmented intelligence.

Let's elaborate further on this concept. As Kevin Kelly mentioned in his latest book *The Inevitable*,[2] animals are good at certain dimensions of intelligence. A squirrel can remember the exact location of several thousand acorns for years, a feat that surpasses human memory. So in that one type of cognition, squirrels exceed humans. Humans have different dimensions of intelligence that outsmart animals, such as visual, verbal, musical, emotional, logical, bodily, interpersonal, and more.

"Artificial minds already exceed humans in certain dimensions," wrote Kelly in his aforementioned *Wired* article. "Your calculator is a genius in math; Google's memory is already beyond our own in a certain dimension."

Let's face it, machines are good at computer vision, computer audition, gaming, artificial diagnosis, artistic and design aid, and so on. Even in nature there is not a single mind that can excel in every aspect, but we tend to believe that it will be possible to build a mind that maximizes all dimensions of intelligence. It is difficult to find evidence of this.

1. Kevin Kelly, "The Myth of a Superhuman AI," *Wired* (April 25, 2017), www.wired.com/2017/04/the-myth-of-a-superhuman-ai/
2. Kevin Kelly, *The Inevitable: Understanding the 12 Technological Forces That Will Shape Our Future* (London: Penguin Books, 2017).

Where humans are good, AI is not that good. So we can think about complementary skills. The future of AI does not look like *Terminator* and *Skynet*, but rather as an aid for humans to become smarter, to augment our intelligence.

The concept of artificial intelligence has been around for decades. It's just now reaching its moment of maturity—its tipping point—largely due to recent advancements in machine learning and deep learning, fueled by the enormous amount of data humankind is producing on a daily basis. These developments have emerged as potent drivers of innovation across a number of industries and are powering the rapid acceleration of artificial intelligence investments.

As this new version of AI arrives, bringing with it applications that will affect the way that billions of people live and work, it's important to think beyond the technology and start a new conversation. This conversation will necessarily include the recognition that augmented intelligence and AI's impacts are not solely on the technology side but also in the business arena. This recognition is at the heart of the most important agenda today, which centers on the numerous parts of our world that will have to adapt, from products to organizations to corporate culture and more.

It's not an entirely unfamiliar agenda. In the recent past, digital innovation has reset many of the traditional boundaries around the way we interact with one another and with businesses. Innovation has pushed large enterprises out of their comfort zone to make a conscious effort to transform themselves from digital followers to digital leaders. Looking ahead, the winners in business will not only be judged by their playbook of assorted technologies, but by how they leverage augmented intelligence within their field.

But there is a big gap between knowing where the next big technology disruption is about to happen and being able to take real advantage of it.

Many manufacturing companies have disappeared, and similarly, many airlines are gone. The same happened with the railroad, as multiple railway companies have disappeared. The pattern was similar: a technological disruption, followed by an investment rush. The return on capital over time in all cases, however, was negative. But many related industries flourished because of these disruptions that included insurance companies, rail manufacturers, airplane manufacturers, road builders, financial services, etc.

Today there are more than 4,000 AI start-ups, according to Angel List.[3] Their valuations are on the very high end, averaging $4.9M USD each, and their investments are enormous. Each of these AI companies have created their own unique platforms. But many will be gone within the next few years.

Company executives must recalibrate themselves and recognize what AI can do for their businesses—and what it can't do. Some of the most important landmarks to reach, mentally, are as follows.

First, we must recognize the strengths of AI and learn about the technology so that it ceases to be a path filled with dread. Let's realize that AI will not put nearly everyone out of work, won't destroy the middle class, and won't, as some would have it, bring an end to the world.

Second, let's focus on solving business problems and not get hung up on the underlying technology. As businesses push forward to boost efficiency and competitiveness, it's critical for them to examine the ways in which AI can improve the

3. Angel List, "Artificial Intelligence Startups" (January 31, 2018), angel.co/artificial-intelligence

entire system. As new digital initiatives take hold and start transformation across the enterprise, more managers must take on the responsibility required to sustain and keep moving these initiatives ahead. The pace of technological change is rapid, and many of today's innovations will be irrelevant tomorrow.

But AI isn't one of them. It will no doubt figure centrally as businesses continue to push for greater efficiency, effectiveness, and customer experience across the enterprise. Smart companies will pursue at least one goal related to AI this year. In fact, around 81 percent of Fortune 500 CEOs list artificial intelligence and machine learning as either very or extremely important for their company's future.[4]

Of course, past experiences with cutting-edge technology have taught us that transformative change takes time. We know that many early AI initiatives will present challenges and many will fail. Just as certainly, we know that commitment to AI will pay off in the long run.

AI is the new disruptor and it's time to get comfortable with the technology and all of its manifestations. The question we need to be asking is not whether we need to invest in AI, but rather, how we do it. Think about which aspects of your business you can improve with AI. Follow that agenda and you will find rewards—if you stay the course of the transformation, if you remain committed to observing behavior, and if you make changes for the good and unlock value from this new technological disruption.

Our goal with this book is to provide you with a primer and strategic guide to these game-changing technologies of AI, machine learning, and augmented intelligence so you can pave a path of initiatives with your company and realize its full potential.

---

4. Alan Murray, "Fortune 500 CEOs See A.I. as a Big Challenge," *Fortune*, (June 2017), fortune.com/2017/06/08/fortune-500-ceos-survey-ai/

INTRODUCTION

Artificial intelligence (AI) has been percolating for years in the minds and hearts of techies, novelists, moviemakers, politicians, and probably you. Whenever we imagined an entity developed by humans that assists, advises, or partners with us—from the automaton Talos in ancient Greece or the artificial being known as Golem in mystic Judaism to the sentient computer HAL 9000 or any other constructed "companion"—we are venturing into the realm of AI.

Trending strongly today, AI is ever present in business and technology magazines, strategies, TED talks, software companies, start-ups, and mass media.

More often than not, artificially created beings have been relegated to monsters created by petty humans who wish to play the role of a powerful deity. It is also worth noting that in many stories, the creations—think Frankenstein, Terminator, or *The Simpsons'* Funzo—turn against their human creators, which has contributed to an undertone of fear with regard to AI.

We still encounter traces of this negative current in many

of our partners, prospects, and customers—and regardless of the hype-induced pressure, the verticals they operate in, and the budget they have, some still linger in this fatalistic pessimism. More apprehensive views of AI lean toward, "AI is going to eat up my industry" or "we'll soon be out of jobs," while others are eager adopters, lamenting "I wish I had the money/talent/support . . ."

The concepts explored in this book complement the methodologies and practices we outlined in our previous book, *The Never Ending Digital Journey.* Our first book focused on the talent, team structure, relevant information, and methodologies required to carry out a digital transformation. It captured much of our fundamental thinking about how we explore and traverse the digital experience with our customers and partners. We've helped many organizations and businesses, big and small, surf the wave of digital renovation so they can bring greater value as they connect with customers and employees in a continuous digital journey.

We consider the topics covered in our earlier book central to helping shape and forge bonds between a brand and its customer or consumers. The integration of AI with our digital transformation methodologies will help support and enhance a digital collaborative culture that leverages small groups of pods as they build next-generation solutions for customers. Fundamental to our distinctive approach is having designers work alongside engineers seamlessly to help spur innovation and drive successful projects and engagements with customers.

Also, by harnessing AI technologies, employees will have more potential as they embrace agile cycles and become part of an experiential journey. AI brings a whole new dimension and set of capabilities that complement and enrich digital journey approaches so clients can tap into the full effect of the digital transformation, all while striking a balance between insight and action.

The magnitude of digital changes underway in business is immense. The expectations of digital products are also extremely imposing. Software development has changed, and the lifecycle in what we describe as an "omnirelevant approach" is to build and think of each build as a mini experiment from which one learns, and which in turn loops back to influence the ongoing design process. In doing so, we embrace technology platforms as "touch points," which lay out an overall experience that leverages data to predict behaviors. We then adapt these touch points with the ultimate aim of delighting, thus humanizing technology.

Our all-digital society leverages an assortment of advanced technologies to reach consumers, penetrate their world, and deliver a persuasive message more effectively. In this new landscape, where technology and Millennials are synonymous, poorly conceived and delivered unilateral digital marketing campaigns are viewed as intrusive and impersonal. Twenty years ago, software's use within organizations was limited to companies' corporate process optimization. Now, software underpins nearly every function in every industry and has become critical to survival.

The future of digital engagement with consumers demands uniqueness and personalization, all of which will surely be enhanced through the application of AI technologies.

Today's digital-native customers are deeply enmeshed in the computing experiences they've been engaged with since their first swipe on an iPad or Android device. One only has to look back a couple of decades to realize how our digital experiences have been transformed. Think about how we used to plan itineraries and book reservations for travel. Before the Internet reshaped the travel experience, everything was done by phone and regular mail. A person would call up or visit a travel agent and discuss their itinerary for a trip they were planning. The travel agent would have limited access to commercial airline reservation systems and that would start the process as the agent asked a series of questions to shape the trip details. Contrast that to today's experience, where consumers have at their fingertips access to multiple airline carriers' schedules, hotels, rental cars, trains, and other modes through an Internet connection on a mobile device or computer that optimizes and sorts for price in a few seconds.

Now consider the addition of AI technologies and how they will transform and deepen these consumer experiences.

Writers and futurists have said that the next phase of the Digital Revolution will bring new methods of combining technology with the creative industries, such as media, fashion, music, entertainment, education, literature, and the arts. But in order for businesses to avoid playing catch-up to a fast moving digital world, companies need to embrace approaches that are agile, user friendly, and adaptive. One well-known example of a start-up taking this approach is Uber. The company began with a simple premise based on user experience: Customers wanted to get a taxi to their door or business without making a phone call. An Uber car shows up where the customer is and within a predicted time frame, and the customer can track its progress and doesn't need any additional interaction for payment. As the car approaches, customers can see its progress on their mobile device in a way that helps ease anxiety wondering whether the car is close or not. This kind of positive user experience builds momentum and a community following that rallies around its "friction-free experience."

The new digital imperative as outlined above is all about staying connected to our human senses in the digital world being created, and thereby experiencing the same powerful emotions we feel in our physical environments. Playing to the strengths of our human senses in a digital world is akin to building the digital journey based on observation and adaptation. Without the ability to process and customize the journey, our digital experience is compromised and undermined, creating friction and other unintended inefficiencies in the overall flow of the digital journey, which makes customers feel as though they're stuck in a world of backlogs and bottlenecks, instead of one of continuous and fluid movement.

Our aim with *The Never Ending Digital Journey* and *Embracing the Power of AI* is to demystify, educate, and ultimately help everyone think with a data-driven mindset, identifying opportunities for how AI can be leveraged to build disruptive new solutions. We will guide you gently, however, since there is prior experience required. Our main purpose is to enable meaningful conversations that are deep enough so that you can leverage your newfound knowledge on a strategic level.

So, what can you expect from this guide?

First, to understand the terminology, hence, to differentiate **AI** from **Machine Learning** (ML), **Deep Learning** (DL), and **Data Science**. Understanding these concepts and their boundaries, however fuzzy, will help you better understand what AI really means. This is the first step to not being afraid of AI.

Second, we want you to understand why this is not just another assemblage of hype—AI is here to stay, and all the conditions are ripe for it to come to fruition now (or yesterday, as we like to say in software). We'll explain what stalled AI in the past (the so-called winters) and what the prevailing enablers are (which happen to be the new reality for software in general) that will make this technology an ever-after.

Third, we will give you the conceptual tools to discern the fiction and the hype from the reality, by getting to know a bit of the cutting-edge developments in the field. Our motto is to "demystify in order to get an intuitive grasp of AI," which will indeed provide you with some insights on the practical applications that can be used today, as well as guide and inspire on what opportunities may look like and give you the confidence to structure projects, understanding what kind of technology to leverage and why.

Fourth, we will show you a wide variety of technologies currently at your disposal. And while this is not meant to be a deep technical guide, it will offer a way of making sense of all the different technologies available to help you understand which is appropriate for your needs.

Last but not least, we will provide extensive current examples, as well as some philosophical, moral, and ethical concerns that are important when discussing a technology that can so greatly benefit humanity but has the potential to also be harmful.

The distinction between "business" and "technology" is always a tricky one to balance. With AI, we must understand that while we care about the business, unless we get into some technical detail, we are contributing to the hype. We will, therefore, delve into technical terms—to get you acquainted or spark your curiosity.

So, without further ado, let's dive into the world of AI.

EMBRACING
the POWER *of*
AI

PART I

THE NEW FRONTIER

OVERVIEW
The New Frontier

The branch of computer science known as artificial intelligence (AI) has quickly become synonymous with the future of computing. It involves many different disciplines of science, but, simply put, is all about adding the characteristics of intelligence to make computing systems sentient. Building learning capabilities into computing systems involves a series of techniques known as machine learning, where complex algorithms with large amounts of data enable machines to learn and anticipate problems and patterns. This chapter will look at the different types of machine learning, introduce the concepts of deep learning and neural networks, and discuss the ways in which data is utilized to enable AI.

CHAPTER I
AI and Other Buzzwords

The first step in making sense of this whole universe is pinning many of the keywords to their respective concepts. We don't need a clear-cut, black-and-white definition, since that is not really possible, but we can at least define some ideas, however fuzzy their thresholds may be. And so, we begin with the buzzwords.

ARTIFICIAL INTELLIGENCE

Artificial intelligence is the idea that machines can be built with an intelligence comparable to that of a human. It is not a concept necessarily linked to software or computers. In fact, it is a much older concept. Since we don't want to get too philosophical at this point, let's just keep it simple and say that AI, as it pertains to us, is a practical field of computer science dedicated to building systems that have certain characteristics of intelligent entities. These characteristics are not required to be explicitly programmed for every possible issue of casuistry.

What makes an entity "intelligent" then? That is not so easily defined, not with computer science or any other field that studies the question. We could even argue that intelligence is not really well understood, on either a philosophical or a scientific basis; hence, we have ill-defined, context-specific, and narrow definitions.

For now, suffice it to say that an important aspect of intelligence is the ability to learn, so we could argue that AI is not possible unless machines are able to learn. Elaborating on this premise, the following characteristics for an artificial intelligence could be considered:

- **contextual:** taking into account the environment and situation when defining the behavior
- **adaptive:** changing as conditions do, in a dynamic way
- **stateful:** having a memory and understanding a series of past events in context, and remembering what has been learned
- **reflexive:** improving with experience, which does not necessarily mean that it can "think" about itself, but rather that it modifies its behavior based on its experiences

COGNITIVE COMPUTING

What is the difference between cognitive computing and AI? Both concepts have been used interchangeably, and in fact, the idea of cognitive computing had a role in the revival of AI.

There is a very thin line separating the concepts of cognition and intelligence in general. They are very much related, but are not exactly the same. For the sake of argument, cognition can be thought of as the mental process by which a human learns, remembers, and perceives the world. Intelligence, on the other hand, is the ability to understand what is perceived, learned, and remembered.

The term *cognitive computing* served as the springboard to present a set of developments, in particular with IBM's question-answering computer system known as Watson. So, coming up with a new, closely related term, served both as a differentiation and as a strategy for making sure the message was heard. Leveraging that with a concerted PR effort was enough to make the term stick, and thus reflect favorably on AI in the market.

As it stands today, the term *cognitive* is often tagged on to a sophisticated service that integrates a whole array of readily available functions, such as Azure Cognitive Services, Watson, and others. The term has now morphed into the combined term *cognitive services*.

ARTIFICIAL GENERAL INTELLIGENCE

Artificial *general intelligence* (AGI) is another term you may have heard. AGI can be thought of as AI that is not purposely built for a narrowly defined task, but rather to be able to do many things in a similar way a human would. The moment some AI is able to modify and improve itself recursively, as a human would, is what is considered the *singularity*, or the moment after which computers would forever surpass human capacity. Often, when we engage in futurology, we envision a world of artificial general intelligence sending us straight to our demise—think *Terminator* or *Ultron.*

Within the AI community, some are preoccupied with the potentially destructive nature of AGI. Advocates of this doomsday vision claim that since machines have exponential capabilities to scale up, once they have reached a certain level of intelligence, humanity will face this *singularity.* That is the day that AI becomes exponentially more intelligent than humans. Elon Musk, for example, is quoted as saying, "I have exposure to the most cutting edge AI, and I think people should be really concerned by it. AI is a fundamental risk to the existence of human civilization, and I don't think people fully appreciate that."[1]

On the other hand, we have advocates like computer scientist and AI visionary Andrew Ng[2] and Facebook founder Mark Zuckerberg,[3] who have a more practical perspective, suggesting that the singularity, while not impossible, is still quite far away. The facts are (to the best of our knowledge) that in terms of advancements in the AI field, practical applications of AI are not general, but rather specific for a certain task. This means that we might have an AI that can beat a human playing Go, but not one that can wipe out humanity.

1. Elon Musk, National Governors Association, "Summer Meeting—Ahead of the Curve," YouTube video (July 2017), www.youtube.com/watch?v=2C-A797y8dA
2. Andrew Ng, "AI Is the New Electricity," YouTube video (June 2017), www.wsj.com/video/andrew-ng-ai-is-the-new-electricity/56CF4056-4324-4AD2-AD2C-93CD5D32610A.html
3. Mark Zuckerberg, "Entreprenuers," CNBC (November 30, 2017), www.cnbc.com/2017/11/30/why-facebook-ceo-mark-zuckerberg-thinks-the-optimists-are-successful.html

ARTIFICIAL NARROW INTELLIGENCE

There are many proponents that believe the singularity is simply not possible, in part because we don't fully grasp how it is we understand and learn, nor do we know how to impart consciousness. So, for now, the only AI possible is limited in its breadth and focus, which is known as *narrow AI* or *weak AI*.

Narrow AI refers to AI that is focused on one narrow task. Examples include computer vision, speech processing, music generation (or sound generation in a more general way), and playing Alpha Go or poker.

While you might be thinking that speech recognition is not really a specific task, but rather a general task, the exercise encompasses several components, which can include converting speech to text, generating speech, extracting emotion, and so on. Therefore, it's actually an array of very specific tasks gathered together within a grossly undefined bundle. It does encompass, in most cases, tools and algorithms for natural language understanding, but that too is contingent on the specific application.

NATURAL LANGUAGE UNDERSTANDING

For those paying close attention, we mentioned natural language understanding (NLU), but what is it? You may have heard natural language processing (NLP) in the past. You could use the terms interchangeably and most likely no one will get hurt (at least we hope not), but note that some consider there to be a slight difference.

In a nutshell, NLU or NLP endeavor to make computers understand human language and communication. In the early days of AI, this was thought to be simple, but, as it turns out, it is extremely complicated—NLU is one of the most challenging things for a machine to do, because human communication is not straightforward. It's a complex web of random, disordered, emotional, conflicting, often ironic exchange in which context is everything. NLP techniques have been applied for decades, and there have been great advances in the field. And yes, in case you are wondering, NLU and NLP are forms of AI.

Basically, language understanding can be thought of as follows: The capacity to "process" is a requisite for "understanding," but the opposite does not hold. So NLU aims to go a step further in extracting context, intention, and desired action. Do those terms feel familiar now?

OTHER

The field of artificial intelligence has been approached from several diverse initiatives, and many have evolved at different rates.

Historically, we have seen approaches like fuzzy logic (a type of logic based on the idea that logical statements are not only true or false, as in Boolean logic, but on degrees of truth), evolutive algorithms (algorithms that use heuristics to solve optimization tasks by imitating some aspects of natural evolution, combining characteristics of "good" solutions and allowing "fitness" to determine "goodness" and survival), search and optimization (algorithms that permit efficient searching over possible solution spaces), cellular automatas (algorithms based on the state of a collection of shapes arranged in a grid, called cells, that evolve with time), or agent-based models (the study of how local logic and interactions generate an emergent complex behavior, system-wide), and so on.

They all are aspects of AI, but given the performance and notoriety of approaches based on deep learning (DL)—more on this in the next chapter—these traditional approaches have mostly fallen out of fashion. Many complex arrays of algorithms rely on these techniques still, but the core of AI is now primarily focused on machine and deep learning.

CHAPTER 2
Machine Learning

Now that we've discussed the top-level buzzwords, let's get into the main set of approaches in which most of those technologies are implemented.

INTUITIVE NOTION

Machine learning (ML) is the practice of using algorithms to enable machines to make a determination or prediction based on prior data. Some of those algorithms are highly complex, especially with the recent developments and advancements of artificial neural networks, which we'll describe in a moment.

The idea of a computer learning without being *explicitly programmed* is the basis of machine learning. We don't tell the computer what to do on a given scenario prescriptively, but rather expose it to many different instances of different scenarios, and we let the machine define the parameters of the algorithm. Thus, we say, it has "learned."

In this sense, learning is inspired by human capabilities, whereby a person can extract a rule, pattern, or make sense of the information, instead of just repeating what it has seen, and adapt to new, different cases. Therein lies the power of learning, based on memory, but on a different level.

Machine learning techniques have been deployed through the decades, and there are hundreds of examples of practical applications. And in the same way that there are many ways for a human being to learn, it is not surprising that there have been many developments in the ways in which a machine can learn. There are numerous specific techniques (or algorithms) that we will explore in Chapter 11, but they mostly fall under one (or more) of the following mechanics: supervised, unsupervised, and reinforcement learning.

SUPERVISED, UNSUPERVISED, AND REINFORCEMENT LEARNING

While there are many training schemes or specific logics, there are broad classes on how we define the objective, the context, and the information available when training an algorithm.

Supervised learning is a kind of *directed* learning. You can think of it as learning by example—for instance, instruction given by a tutor to the student (in this case the algorithm). These exercises have an expected output, and the answer can be right, wrong, somewhat close, etc.

- In supervised learning, algorithms learn from data for which we know the output. Training data is labeled.

- Regressions and classification are all examples of supervised learning schemes.

- A typical example is that if I show the algorithm a million pictures of a cat, with an explicit tag that says it's a cat, and a million pictures of "not-cat," the machine can learn to discriminate. Then, upon showing an unknown picture, we can ask whether it's a cat or not.

Unsupervised learning on the other hand, is like having a bucket full of Legos. There is no explicit or expected outcome—just go do something. You can separate the pieces by color, stack them by shape, build a castle, whatever you want; there is no objective but the one you set for yourself.

- In unsupervised learning, we do not have or use a "ground truth" (a.k.a. an expected variable output) for our training data, so we let the algorithm discover relationships or patterns in the data.

- Clustering, dimensionality reduction, and word embeddings are examples of unsupervised learning schemes.

- Let's say I have a lot of data about a group of customers, including things like their age, income, annual spending, frequency of purchase, recency, and more. I might want to know if there are "groups" of customers that behave alike, but since I have many different pieces of information about each of them (known as "features"), a histogram won't do, as they might be differentiated by a conjunction of them, and doing arbitrary cuts *(if they spend more than 1 MM, they are high rollers)* does not add any new information. I can tell the algorithms to *group them by similarity*, giving me "clusters" of customers. Self-segmentation to the rescue!

Reinforcement learning is like a version of the young Spartans who were given spears, helmets, and shields, and delivered into the wilderness (of data in this case). The ones who survived came back and told the others what they think helped them. Some, when it was their turn, followed closely the lessons learned from those who succeeded. Others wanted to explore new ways. Over time, *knowledge* was built, guiding the following generations.

- With reinforcement learning, we have a broad understanding of what a good final outcome means, or at least we have a way of comparing them (with an appropriate metric or KPI) to know which one is better. We have to make many decisions in the different steps or stages to get to any outcome, and we do not know precisely which logic or criteria we should use.

- Q Learning, Deep Policy Learning, or (for some) generative adversarial networks are examples of reinforcement learning.

- I want to win at Go (or chess or something else), but no single move is by itself better than the rest. It depends on what the board looks like, what the opponent can do, and every move I make henceforth! What I need is a way to assess which move is appropriate on whatever situation I find myself in. I will only know if my criteria were good or bad when the game ends.

NEURAL NETWORKS AND DEEP LEARNING

In the context of AI and machine learning, there is quite a lot of buzz about neural networks as the technique of choice. It makes sense to take a look at why that may be.

Artificial neural networks (ANN) is yet another way of doing machine learning. They are inspired by our understanding of the biology of our brains and all those interconnections between neurons. The idea behind neural networks (NN), then, is pretty simple: mimic how the human brain, or more specifically, the neurons, work. It should be noted, however, that NNs mimic what researchers understand of the way neurons work in a very reductionist, bottom-up stance. We cannot say that a brain is just a huge ANN. But the other way around does work, in the sense that as scientists gain more insights about the brain, ANN researchers try to leverage those mechanisms in their own work.

Any NN is organized as a directed graph, or complex array of neurons. The neuron is the little machine that takes input and gives processed output. In mathematical terms, each neuron represents a nonlinear function of its weighted inputs (whether the beginning of the algorithm or the output of some other neurons). From the same set of inputs, you could stack neurons with a different set of weights, forming a sort of layer. Then you could stack the layers and create your neural network.

In the early days, NNs were abandoned because they were considered numerically unsuitable and intractable—simply put, it was considered impossible to build a practical, real-world solution with them. In recent years, thanks to many factors (which we will discuss in Chapter 5), NNs became a viable approach to solve ML problems. Furthermore, NN began to have more and more layers, becoming "deep" and giving rise to the term *deep learning*. Deep learning has enabled many more practical applications of machine learning and, by extension, of AI in general.

When you start stacking layers in ANNs, or structure the network so that it takes several neurons in any single path to go from the overall input to the final output, it grows deep. It gains the capacity to learn more complex representations of the data. But when you start providing that network with some specialized structures (for instance, to more easily leverage spatial or temporal structure in the way the data is fed), the capacity to train the network increases. And then we are talking about deep learning.

There are a lot of trade-offs in going deep. On one hand, it has enormous potential and learning power. On the other, it needs unreasonable amounts of data and computing power.

When talking about DL, here are some things you need to consider:

- Deep learning is still young and moving at a rapid pace. Every other month, great breakthroughs or applications are published and implemented. Nevertheless, some savvy thinkers and experts argue that DL is not the silver bullet for machine learning and AI. Some consider that the approach of just throwing more data and more computing power to an algorithm is not enough to solve complex problems that require other types of approaches.

- Graphic processing units (GPU), familiar to the gaming community, can perform parallel processing and complex matrix and math operations very fast, which is at the heart of DL. Because of this, GPUs have been adopted, adapted, and leveraged for deep learning.

- Tensor processing units (TPU) are Google's attempt at creating DL chips with a dedicated architecture. While great advances have been made, there is still a ways to go. For example, there is still a problem with optimizing sparse matrix multiplications (very difficult problem to overcome), which has a huge impact on DL.

- There are many ways the neurons and the layers of a deep neural network (DNN) can be arranged. These arrangements are called the NN architecture. Depending on the task at hand, different

architectures have been found to better handle the
challenge. For example, to do image processing,
convolutional neural networks (CNN) perform
very well.

- The most used neural network architectures are:
  feedforward (FF) neural network, convolutional
  neural network (CNN), recurrent neural network

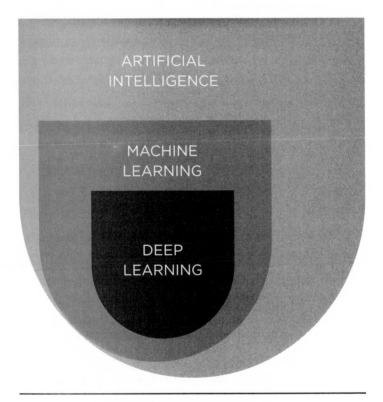

FIGURE 2.1: *Relationship between AI, ML, and DL*

(RNN), and long short-term memory (LSTM), which is the king of RNN.

To visualize the relationship between DL, ML, and AI, see figure 2.1. Note that while we discussed the division of machine learning in three different approaches, they all apply to deep learning, so we don't include those distinctions for the sake of clarity.

Why is machine learning so close to the edge of AI? That is not a coincidence. In Chapter 11 we'll discuss some of the building blocks and algorithms used to build AI. They were not produced solely for AI, but are rather the outcomes of many disciplines, such as mathematics, statistics, data mining, and others. So, while in this context we are intent on making the machine learn, many of those methods have been created and used in the past for other things.

CHAPTER 3
Data Science

We have frequently mentioned the word *data* and have indicated that ML and AI rely heavily on it to be of any actual use. In this chapter, we'll put the spotlight on data and look at the ways in which it is utilized to enable AI- and ML-backed solutions. We will also review the activities, profiles, and approaches of data usage as it relates to AI and ML.

AREA OF FOCUS

Here, we are going to explore data science and the kind of work required in an AI setting, which needs to be addressed in the team, whether as a profile or as a compound activity.

In a noncommercial setting, or in academia, the focus could be shifted to the design and improvement of particular algorithms. Whenever it interacts with consumers (internal or external), the focus on the data becomes even more important.

FIGURE 3.1: *This figure shows the complexity of relationships of interdisciplinary fields relevant to data science.*

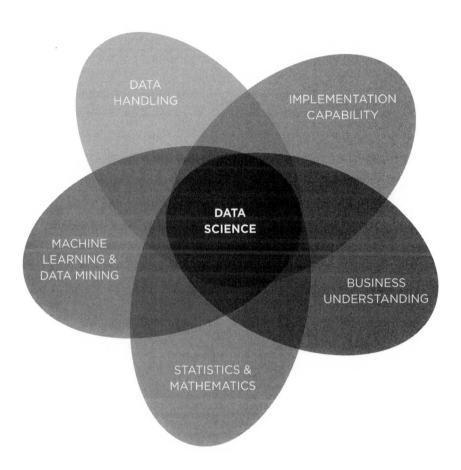

The objective of data science in this regard, then, is to be able to inquire and provide answers or solutions to fundamental questions about its usage: *What data should be used? What does the data mean, in terms of new knowledge? Is the available data appropriate for the use-case? How can I understand the outcome of the algorithms? Are there implicit biases that need to be taken into account? Am I getting the kind of output that I need?*

It's about dealing with uncertainty, with regard to the input, the output, the process, the implications, and so on.

To best utilize the data, the following things need to happen:

PROBLEM FRAMING

- Define the immediate use of the knowledge gained from the algorithms and how the problem needs to be defined in mathematical terms in order to be solvable.
- As the ol' operations-research mantra goes, having a problem well defined is half the solution!

DATA UNDERSTANDING AND PROCESSING

- Collect the data, analyze the data, understand the data, and prepare the data for algorithm training and evaluation.
- This step is rarely simple. Navigating through gigabytes or terabytes of data is not an easy endeavor. And, of course, it is not only a matter of quantity but also of quality. It is the task of the data scientist to deal with all of these challenges.

AI AND ML ALGORITHMS TWEAKING

- Train the algorithms: Feed the algorithms with lots of examples.

- Test the algorithms: Show the algorithms new data that they have never seen.

- Validate the outcome: Validate that the output of the algorithm given the new data makes sense.

- Evaluate: Check that the computational cost of getting the outcome is affordable in a production (real-world) environment. Perform sensitivity analysis.

The process we have just described is hardly a linear process. In practice, it can feel almost chaotic in the sense that a lot of back and forth from the different stages in the process usually occurs.

In conclusion, data science should be thought of as a field of study that's situated at the intersection of statistics, mathematics, machine learning, subject matter ("business") understanding, and computer science.

PART II

TIMING

OVERVIEW
Timing

AI has become the new reality in both the business and consumer worlds. Its arrival signals the opportunity for businesses to start benefiting from this new wave of technology and embrace its power to drive innovation. The push is happening across several different areas of development that range from data availability and management, affordable computing power, data collection tools, and data analysis and processing. Once harnessed, AI's new technologies will help businesses discover emerging opportunities, which will help drive a reinforcement loop (or virtuous cycle) for the development and growth of AI technology.

CHAPTER 4
AI Winters

If some of the techniques we have discussed so far are not necessarily bleeding-edge new (for example, ANNs have been in development for decades), why weren't they a hit in the past? What changed? How do we know that this time they are here to stay?

SEASONS

Artificial intelligence has been a dream and a goal of computer science for quite some time, and throughout the decades there were several advances in capabilities, research, and understanding of the topic. Applications were even developed and deployed. After most of these advances, the initial enthusiasm gave way to disappointment and opinions about the factual impossibility of the task at hand.

You may remember Deep Blue beating Kasparov at chess, and may wonder about how long ago that happened. Were any practical applications for real-world problems created? We can still say that it was a great breakthrough in improving the methods and capabilities used at the time, but the payout was short-lived. And if we go further back in time, we can see a pattern: breakthrough in AI, some hype, some funding, development, sometimes deployment, and then a sudden drop in activity and excitement. A valley of disillusionment. Those extended periods of nothingness are called AI winters.

The reason for those winters are somewhat clear. A common pattern emerges wherein a promising breakthrough was usually followed by great disillusionment, which dampened the possibilities for new funds and investing. Let's discuss an example.

In 1954, a Georgetown-IBM experiment demonstrated the successful translation of sixty Russian sentences to English. At the time, automatic translation from Russian to English was a sweet spot since the United States and Russia were in the middle of the Cold War. The demo was considered very successful—the sixty sentences were fed to the algorithm and the translation was perfect. This triggered funding for a generalized automated approach of translation from Russian to English.

Many companies and agencies tried to tackle this daunting challenge and failed miserably. One way to assess the capabilities of translation is to do it in a whole circle, back and forth from the origin to the target language. In this case, a phrase in English would be translated into Russian, and the Russian translation would then be translated into English.

In most of those systems, when fed the phrase "The spirit is willing, but the flesh is weak" to translate into Russian and back to English, the output would be akin to "The whiskey is strong, but the meat is rotten."

It might seem that for a syntactic word-for-word translation, the result is not that bad, but imagine trying to translate a whole letter or book—the result would be so scrambled it would not make sense. In the end, the automated translation could not be trusted, not beyond a novelty and definitely not for sensitive matters.

This example shows the type of disillusionment faced when trying to tackle complex challenges without the proper means and conditions. Why did this failure happen? Because a carefully crafted and constrained AI system worked very well within the boundaries and context for which it was built. But as soon as it was tested outside those boundaries, it failed completely.

The application side of the failed experiment was one component in the resulting lack of trust in the technology. On the technical side, there were concerns as well.

When the first artificial neural networks (ANN) were created in 1958, in the form of the perceptron (or an NN with one hidden layer), it was mathematically impossible to generate an exclusive-or (XOR) logic, laying waste to the potential of the technique. Furthermore, there was influential research by Marvin Minsky and Seymour Papert in 1969 that exposed two main problems with ANN at that time. The first one we just described, and the second one was that computers didn't have enough processing power to effectively handle the work required by large neural networks.

By 1975, the process of backpropagation was invented, making it possible for ANNs to learn multilayer models, or solve the XOR problem. The problems of vanishing gradients (the inability to learn on deep representations), shift variance, and intolerance to deformations arose. And so the story goes.

After this history, you might be wondering, why support AI now? What if an AI winter were to drop down on us again? If these types of boom-and-bust cycles have happened several times in the past, why should we invest and bet on AI this time?

We'll explore the conditions, along with many prominent cases, that make us believe the cycle is broken and the winters are gone for good.

CHAPTER 5
Ripe for Blooming

Now that we've seen how the AI winters evolved in the past, we will explore the changes and conditions that make artificial intelligence a suitable and sustainable technology moving forward. What are those conditions?

MATURITY

Let's think about the different dimensions that work as enablers of artificial intelligence: data, processing power, access, and technical prowess.

On the data front, we live in a radically different world from decades past in at least two ways. Internet ubiquity is one. The mobile revolution is the other. Billions of devices are connected to the web—not just laptops and desktop computers, but also phones, cars, home-assistant devices, and many others.

Available data sources (very active ones at that) broadcast all sorts of information about their users and their workings. Furthermore, Internet of things (IoT) devices close the loop, acting as both sensors and actuators, bridging the gap between the digital and the physical.

This means that on a daily basis the amount of data generated, processed, stored, and made available is getting bigger, faster, and more varied. This trend does not show any sign of slowing down. In fact, it's accelerating. You can think of what is called Zuckerberg's Law, or the Social Sharing Law, as the counterpart of Moore's Law, stating that people are expected to share twice as many "things" (status updates, pictures, interactions, etc.) every year over the prior one.

To handle that, we have storage that is cheaper than ever, bigger than ever, and all kinds of tools that enable managing all that data at the required speed and handling all the different varieties of data, which are ever more available and mature.

This enabler actually has a name, one that has been a buzzword of its own for several years now. Does **Big Data** ring a bell?

Let's visit the processing power now. Deep Blue was, physically speaking, a huge supercomputer. The first time it played chess again Kasparov, it actually failed. For the rematch, a lot of computing power was added. The lads at IBM, with deep pockets akin to IBM's budget, were able to develop that monstrous machine, but it's hard to imagine a small garage start-up being able to invest all those millions to build something like that—or a couple of independent researchers, or a small experimental unit within another business.

Nowadays, graphics processing units (GPU) are available at a reasonable price if you want to set up an in-house server to do some sort of AI. The same way that many big data developments tackled commodity off-the-shelf (COTS) hardware, pursuing high-performance computing, AI shifted to leveraging graphic cards (Nvidia being the major player). They were developed for the throughput requirements of graphics rendering and became a cheap way of accessing an enormous parallel processing capacity.

There were major changes in off-premise venues. Enter cloud computing, which enabled everyone to access an AI-ready infrastructure in a very cost-efficient way, paying as they go, instead of buying lots of hardware (and lowering the entrance barrier to that kind of hardware by not needing to know how to set up a private cluster). Combined with GPUs, you could access a whole array of high-performance servers for a very competitive price. In case you missed it, we stumbled upon another buzzword: **Cloud Computing**.

In terms of access and technical prowess, we can see the open-source movement has achieved an incredible level of maturity and reach. It has allowed access to everything from languages, tools, frameworks, and libraries to online courses and materials, as well as the interplay between academia and open source, building upon and sharing each other's improvements. Tools like TensorFlow, Python, Torch, CNTK, Anaconda, Jupyter, R, and more, make the development and training of algorithms much simpler.

Big tech players are investing heavily in the development of artificial intelligence components that can be leveraged to build "powered by AI" solutions, with such familiar names (or not so much) as IBM's Watson, Microsoft's Azure Cognitive Services, Google Cloud Platform Machine Learning Services,

Amazon ML, Dialogflow (previously known as Api.ai), and so on. We will revisit them in Chapter 9, describing the landscape and the use cases.

With such a promise of economic benefit with reduced amounts of risks, many are investing heavily in the advancements of AI and adopting AI solutions. And the bet is paying off, as many companies are using artificial intelligence not as merely a novelty to show off, but to successfully drive core processes for them. The hype cycle became a virtuous one.

All the aforementioned conditions are strong indicators that artificial intelligence is here to stay and that practical applications of the technology can be leveraged with a huge side note: Artificial intelligence has the power to disrupt business in many layers. We can either grow with it or get displaced from the ecosystem altogether.

On the flip side, this explosion brought myriad start-ups and initiatives competing to find the value proposition, approach, or use case. We are experiencing an artificial intelligence gold rush, with an emergent structure yet to appear.

PART III
FROM MYTH TO MAKING SENSE

OVERVIEW
From Myth to Making Sense

Despite all the hype surrounding artificial intelligence, worthwhile AI projects to date embody simple kinds of tasks that involve going from input A to output B. Successful projects will enhance the experience of accessing and processing information, as well as making decisions, and fundamental to performance is abundant, high-quality, labeled data. Underlying successful projects is how AI helps make any kind of data translatable to any other, which ultimately helps businesses realize the types of initiatives they can tackle and determine the expertise they need for the team from the fields of data science, architecture, and user experience. In addition to the skills, processes, and stages necessary for a successful implementation of an AI project, it is important to also recognize what an AI project is *not*.

CHAPTER 6
Demystifying AI

So far, we have discussed what AI means and why it is a feasible approach to solving real-world problems. But we have not mentioned the practical applications of AI, many of which are currently being deployed, nor have we shown how it is useful in our everyday lives.

PERSPECTIVE

We can take a shortcut to understand the current state of affairs of artificial intelligence "in the wild" with the opinion of Andrew Ng, a leading AI expert:

> *"Surprisingly, despite AI's breadth of impact, the types of it being deployed are still extremely limited. Almost all of AI's recent progress is through one type, in which some input data (A) is used to quickly generate some simple response (B)."*
> — ANDREW NG, *Harvard Business Review*, November 2016

There are two things to highlight from that statement. First, he mentions that the types of AI products deployed are still limited. The deployments are "limited" with regard to the number of tasks and the generalities of what the AI actually accomplishes. This is not to say they are meaningless or irrelevant at all. These accomplishments are huge enablers for companies—aside from also being very cool show-offs. To give a trivial example, compare a machine's capacity to automatically process millions of photos to an army of people doing it manually.

The second point to highlight is the down-to-earth approach to artificial intelligence. It's no longer an impractical field of computer science. There are deployments out there that are already impacting our everyday life, without having to think about it.

Offering some concrete examples to help you visualize the statement, let's use Andrew Ng's notation of Input A, Response B, and the possible application:

- Input A are pictures, and we want a Response B of the type: Are there human faces in the pictures? With this sort of AI, we could build a photo-tagging application.

- Input A are loan applications, and we want a Response B of the type: Will the loan be repaid? With this we could build an AI-powered loan approval application.

- Inputs A are ads and user information, and the Response B we want is: Will the user click on an ad? With this we can build an ultra-targeted online-ads platform (not so alien to our common experience, is it?).

Diving deeper, we can add some more examples:

- We have audio as input, we want the transcript of the audio as an output. With this we can build a speech to text application or take it further to speech recognition.

- Using a sentence, in English for the sake of argument, and expecting the sentence translated to French as an output, we could build a language translation application.

- What about a self-driving car? For that we would have input from cameras and other sensors like light detection and ranging (LIDAR). The type of outputs could be the speed, trajectory, and positions of other cars and objects.

KEY ASPECTS

With all the different possible applications and players getting into AI, what remains to be tackled are the key aspects for a successful AI product and to determine what the key considerations are.

First, successful AI products must be driven by one or both of two fundamental goals: aiding people in **accessing and processing information**, and facilitating **decision-making**. The crucial characteristic shared by both is that AI is treated as technology to supplement, not replace, human capability. Developers and applications that fail to grasp the continued necessity of human participation are doomed to fail, while those that do are poised for sustainable success.

Second, the need of data, which is an unquenchable need. We mentioned in Chapter 5 that there is a growing availability of data and maturity of the tools needed to collect and manage it. Having available data does not necessarily mean it is useful "as-is" to develop artificial intelligence and machine learning. Data "in the wild" is usually not. We also discussed in Chapter 3 the discipline (or profile and role) of data science—to understand the data, clean it, integrate it, process it, and eventually label it for training an algorithm.

Labeled data is at the heart of the majority of current deployments of machine learning. It is the way in which an algorithm can be taught by example which input corresponds to which output. But not just any data will do. It needs to be of good quality if it is going to "teach" anything useful. Quality, in this sense, implies the following:

- **curated** so that no wrong or mistaken data is consumed, and it's processed in a way that makes it suitable for consumption.

- **labeled** so that the expected outcome, or lesson to learn, is present, enabling the most powerful methods at our disposal to be used.

- **balanced**, which means that the sets of characteristics and outcomes are not skewed in a way that constrains generalization or leads to biased assumptions.

- **representative** of the kind of situation we are trying to assess and not a subset or special case. How good would my go-to-the-beach model (see below) be if all the data points come from winter days?

Following an example used by Skiena,[1] let's say you are building a predictive go-to-the-beach model that, depending on several variables, predicts whether people will go to the beach or not as the outcome. In this case you might have an input that looks like this:

Outlook = Sunny,
Temperature = High,
Humidity = High,
Go to the beach = Yes

That input can be labeled as *Beach*.

1. Steven S. Skiena, *The Data Science Design Manual*, Springer (2017), www.springer.com/us/book/9783319554433

Another data point (also known as *datum*) could be as follows:

Outlook = Sunny,
Temperature = Low,
Humidity = Normal,
Go to the beach = No

That can be labeled as *NoBeach*. Having that labeled data is critical to train the model that will make the prediction.

If you remember Chapter 2, you might be wondering, *Why do we need labeled data in the first place? Don't we have unsupervised learning techniques available?* Recalling the difference between supervised and unsupervised methods, we are not trying to see if there is some endogenous structure to the data that we can leverage. We have a specific objective. The trick we want our pony to learn is knowing when to go to the beach. If we don't have the labels, how can we direct him toward them? Without labels, there is no right or wrong answer upfront. Unsupervised techniques would be a helpful approach for exploring the data and making sense out of an untouched (by humans) dataset. But to get a *specific* response, we need *supervised* techniques.

Last but not least, it's important to understand that the current state of the art in artificial intelligence and machine learning enables us to extract useful data out of any kind of "dark" data, or data hidden within a picture, phrase, piece of audio, and so on. That is something that we are seeing being used in social networks, retail, finance, and other industries to extract information from these sources and make it richer.

EXAMPLES

Having a general understanding of the approach, we can now dive a bit further into examples.

IMAGES

A very interesting challenge that can be tackled in an easier way with artificial intelligence is computer vision. Through deep learning algorithms, you can recognize objects and actions in video and pictures, with a process like the one shown in figure 6.1. This is not the first time object recognition has been achieved, since other techniques for image processing also worked in the past, but the accuracy and performance of deep learning techniques have greatly surpassed those approaches, improving beyond human capacities in some domains.

Imagine a piece of software that detects bone fractures on X-rays. The system can be trained to identify healthy bones and fractured bones by being fed tons of X-ray images. The approach in this particular example would be to use supervised learning, by having experts labeling training data. In the later chapters, we will discuss whether this means that the doctor who used to look at the X-rays and diagnose the fracture ceases to have purpose or how it evolves.

Other applications of video processing could be using the feed of cameras placed throughout aisles of a store, and using artificial intelligence to identify customers, count people, or to audit shelves and assess if they need replenishing.

Once again, the key aspect is to build and design the AI

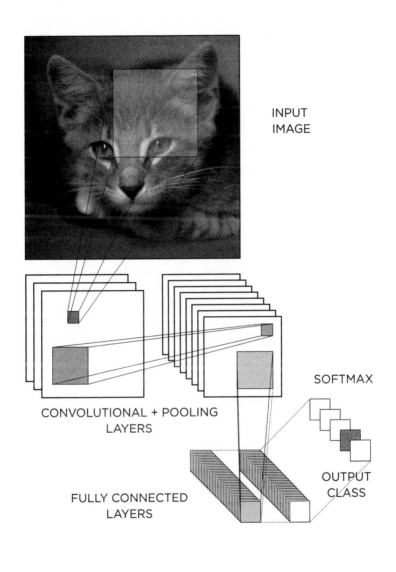

INPUT
IMAGE

SOFTMAX

CONVOLUTIONAL + POOLING
LAYERS

OUTPUT
CLASS

FULLY CONNECTED
LAYERS

FIGURE 6.1: *Image recognition: This is a cat.*

component to aid people and facilitate decision-making. In the examples above, we can imagine improving the shopping experience of a customer or enhancing the work of a store operations team. In the case of the X-rays, the benefits are for the patient and for the doctor as well.

Sounds

The same way deep learning revolutionized image and video processing, audio processing is getting to a level of development that blurs the line between reality and fiction.

Deep learning is enabling devices to detect speech and translate it to text, with a schematic of the process illustrated in figure 6.2. All of the voice-activated services (Alexa, Google Voice, and others) are powered by neural networks and deep learning of some sort.

Referencing Andrew Ng[2] once again, he has long predicted that as speech recognition goes from a 95 percent to 99 percent accuracy rate, it will become a primary way in which we interact with computers. The point he makes is that this 4 percent accuracy gap is the difference between annoyingly unreliable and incredibly useful. Thanks to deep learning, we're finally crossing that threshold. That 4 percent gap is the perceptual difference between an AI that generates a choppy and robotic voice versus one that is smooth and almost indistinguishable from humans.

That is the holy grail of speech recognition with deep learning, but we aren't quite there yet (at least at the time of this writing—time will tell how fast we get there).

2. Andrew Ng, "As speech-recognition accuracy goes from 95% to 99%, we'll go from barely using it to using all the time!" December 15, 2016, Tweet, twitter.com/AndrewYNg/status/809579698883727360

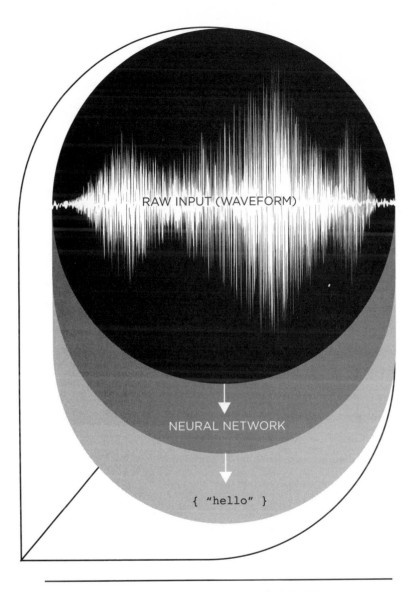

RAW INPUT (WAVEFORM)

NEURAL NETWORK

{ "hello" }

FIGURE 6.2: *Audio processing: Extracted "hello"; from the recorded audio of someone saying "hello" to a string-type variable containing the word "hello."*

As a technical side note, one of the biggest challenges in recognition is that speech varies in speed. One person might say "hello" very quickly and another person might say "h...e...l...l...o..." very slowly, producing a much longer sound file with many more bits of data. Both sound files should be recognized as exactly the same text. Automatically aligning audio files of various lengths to a fixed-length piece of text turns out to be pretty difficult, and it's actually required as part of the training of our models.

Nonetheless, speech recognition is a reality from which companies can seek business opportunities, whether that is gathering more data from their customer relationship, utilizing automation, or providing new ways for users to interact with software.

Natural Language

The last example of AI for media is natural language, as in raw, unprocessed, free-form text that comprises SMSs, tweets, emails, books, and every other origin, including the speech to text apps mentioned earlier.

Dealing with language in text has been part of the traditional research domain of artificial intelligence, though it has seen remarkable improvements with the advent of deep learning, specifically with the recurrent neural network family and combinations thereof (which we will describe later).

One of the capabilities gained would be generating a nonextractive abstract of a text, let's say a long chain of emails. This means that instead of selecting representative words or parts of phrases, it would generate a brand-new text that encompasses the meaning of what has been written in the source material.

This kind of approach has enabled translation apps, as we mentioned before, with an unprecedented reliability through what is called neural machine translation (NMT), a sample of which you may be familiar with if you used Google Translate in the last year.

And in the same way, an extended capacity to do sentiment analysis is available, which can not only say whether a given text has a positive or negative emotion associated with it, but can get into the nuances of the type of emotions we want to map.

Making Data Translucent

We have mentioned dark data, and now we will explain it. When we have tidy data (as in an enterprise data warehouse), it is ready to be consumed by whatever process or analysis we set out to do. Most data is not tidy in this sense. It is opaque. A computer can access all the pixel values within a picture or every bit of a recorded sound wave, but not the face or voice within it. The information is encoded in such a way that is neither easily nor readily available for consumption by algorithms, such as the objects represented in a picture or the overall meaning of a phrase, or the words recorded in a piece of audio, and so on.

The examples of text-to-speech, image recognition, or language translation show the capacity for extraction of that

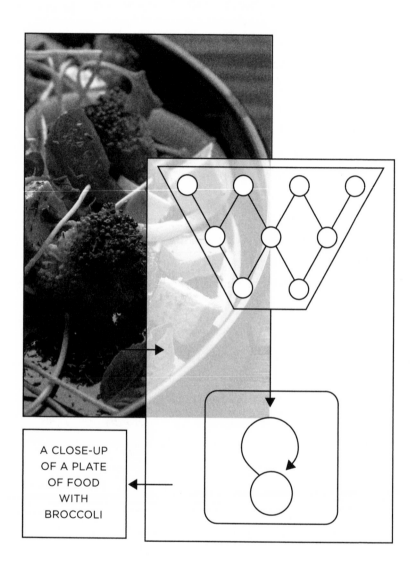

A CLOSE-UP OF A PLATE OF FOOD WITH BROCCOLI

FIGURE 6.3: *Generating a descriptive text from an image.*

information. Through deep learning we also have the capacity to generate that kind of representation, whether it's a text description of a picture, as shown in figure 6.3, or a generative score of music,[3] or speech, and so on. This represents a more general capacity, which is "translating" from one way of representing data to a different one.

We can even go a step further by generating data that never existed, based on arbitrary input, and making it so that it is indistinguishable from a real image. One such example is the groundbreaking Stacked-GANs,[4] from which we can find examples (see figure 6.4) taken from the paper where the pictures were generated from a text description.

This is a big picture. If we can shift from one medium to another, then any kind of data is as valuable as structured data, which has been the lifeblood of machine learning. Making a decision based on structured data was already the forte of machine learning. Deep learning brings this to a new order of magnitude by improving the manageable complexity of the decision and making almost any kind of data readily available!

3. You can check AIVA for some impressive examples.

4. Han Zhang, et al, "StackGAN: Text to Photo-realistic Image Synthesis with Stacked Generative Adversarial Networks" Cornell, December 10, 2016, arXiv:1612.03242v2 [cs.CV]; image extracted from the publication.

TEXT DESCRIPTION	THIS BIRD IS RED AND BROWN IN COLOR, WITH A STUBBY BEAK
256 X 256 STACKGAN	
TEXT DESCRIPTION	A SMALL BIRD WITH VARYING SHADES OF BROWN WITH WHITE UNDER THE EYES
256 X 256 STACKGAN	

FIGURE 6.4: *Generating an image from a description*

THIS BIRD IS
SHORT AND
STUBBY WITH
YELLOW ON
ITS BODY

A BIRD WITH
MEDIUM ORANGE
BILL, WHITE BODY,
GRAY WINGS, AND
WEBBED FEET

THIS SMALL
BLACK BIRD
HAS A SHORT,
SLIGHTLY
CURVED BILL
AND LONG LEGS

A SMALL YELLOW
BIRD WITH A
BLACK CROWN
AND A SHORT,
BLACK, POINTED
BEAK

THIS SMALL BIRD
HAS A WHITE
BREAST, LIGHT
GREY HEAD,
BLACK WINGS
AND TAIL

CHAPTER 7
What Does an AI Project Look Like?

Now that we have seen what AI can be used for, let's take a look at what is needed to execute an AI project. We'll briefly discuss team roles, process, and a brief comparison with other development projects.

You may be familiar with Agile methodologies, especially if you come from a computer science background, and with the idea that a good approach to handle uncertainties is to break them down into smaller chunks, prioritize the user stories with highest ROI, and so on. Enter AI and ML, and the process becomes a bit more complex. Before getting into the details of how to execute these types of projects, let's first discuss the desired team composition.

THE TEAM

In a nutshell, we want a core team that is mature and highly autonomous (part of what we call an *Agile Pod*, or a small, cross-functional, multidisciplinary team that is self-contained and held accountable by metric measurements that show maturity) in a way that can cover the roles of **data science** for data understanding, cleaning, labeling, and algorithmic part; **data architecture** for the management of the data infrastructure, ingestion, storage, processing capacity, and scaling; and **user experience** (which can be focused on service design) in order to design the usage scenarios and establish the touchpoints, the journey, and so on.

But that's not the end of the story. We will also need to add more capabilities to the extended team, which, in our case, can be found within Globant's studio structure, and other teams may have specialists to do so. For example, in order for artificial intelligence to succeed, you need instances of big data to process, whether it's a data platform or data lake or any other shape. Also, cloud computing becomes especially important in AI, as the ability to access information and computing power everywhere and easily is crucial for the effectiveness of the system. Internet of things enables artificial intelligence to be (and act) everywhere, as well as to collect data from sensors. The team would need to expose the AI and ML components through some sort of microservices, web or mobile apps, and integration into an enterprise backend, and, of course, make it available to end users through the appropriate UI.

What about testing? In the next section, you will have a clearer picture of the whole process by which to build an AI/ML solution. Usually all the traditional approaches to testing (functional, manual, automation, performance) apply to these type of projects, with considerations. The testing needs to focus on the end-to-end solution, rather than on the AI/ML component itself. For that component, we will see what the proper approach to testing is.

Last but not least, in our experience, having a clear idea and design from the start of what the end product or project should look like is rare, which means that starting with a full team usually is not a great idea. We can start with a core team (data scientist, data architect, and service designer) to build and discover in the initial phase, before ramping up with all the other profiles. Someone will need to play the product-owner role, and the scope needs to be flexible enough to encompass the discoveries and new use cases that come along the way.

THE PROCESS

Getting a grasp of the business needs is crucial, as is understanding the data sources. Are we thinking the solution centers on user needs or are we putting technology first? Going back to the key aspects discussed in Chapter 6 (see page 73), successful AI products must be driven and designed to help people access and process information, and facilitate decision-making.

That very first issue for the team is problem formulation, during which they will define the business needs to be addressed in a way that is usable, identify the expected outcome, and even more so, how they will use that outcome so as to ensure it's not spurious.

Next comes understanding the data sources—how healthy they are, how to integrate them, and how the team can use them to fulfill the business goal. Given that, the first thing to do is check that we can actually process the data of the client, without regard for speed or complexity, and validate that we can get a suitable business answer. It's not relevant if it's not the best one, since we should make sure that we are doing something that is worth doing. If all these checks go through, we can plan to scale up.

To summarize, the questions that have to be addressed are:

- What data sources are available?

- What is the meaning of the data?

- Do we have enough data?

- How is the data generated and collected?

And there are some other questions that might not be the point in terms of feasibility, but that should be up for discussion since they will empower or undermine the quality of the whole endeavor:

- Is the data that we are using to train the model representative enough?

- Are there any biases we are not factoring out?

- Can the data be used with disclosure, without alienating the end user?

There is another step on handling the data before the algorithm itself, which is called feature engineering and consists of how the data can be combined and modified to make it more significant to the algorithms that are going to consume it. This includes, for instance, squaring variables or multiplying them to allow linear models to model nonlinearities, or more generally applying kernels, performing a Fourier transform to handle the domain frequency to process audio, or passing an image through the SIFT algorithm in order to locate features in images.

While this step is critical in traditional machine learning, it has been shifting into architecture engineering when talking about deep learning, since one of the capabilities of these deep neural networks is learning features by themselves. In that situation, the focus becomes defining an architecture that enables the algorithm to learn the best possible features.

Once we have a clear business goal and a clear understanding of the data, we can then start with the modeling of algorithms. This will include training the algorithms, testing the algorithms, visualizing the outcome, and evaluating it.

Training an algorithm can be likened to training a dog, but millions of times. As trivial as that sounds, the process is as simple as this: You have input data of which you know the expected outcome; you feed the data to the algorithm, which will give an answer back for that data; and you give feedback to the AI, pointing out which answer is right and which one is wrong (more likely: this answer is about "this much" wrong).

The process may seem simple, but executing it effectively and correctly is far from trivial, requiring a lot of focus and effort. We need to define a strategy, otherwise the artificial intelligence can learn unwanted and unforeseen negative behaviors. One heavily touted example happened to Google[1] when image recognition software was fed a photo of an African-American family, and it tagged it as a shrewdness of apes (group of apes). Had that outcome anything to do with

1. James Vincent, "Google 'fixed' its racist algorithm by removing gorillas from its image-labeling tech," *The Verge* (January 12, 2018), https://www.theverge.com/2018/1/12/16882408/google-racist-gorillas-photo-recognition-algorithm-ai.

racism? We will discuss that a bit more in Chapter 13, but the behavior of the AI emerges from the dataset and process used during the training and testing phase.

This stresses how the training part is very important, and therein lies the success of the behavior that you design for it. This is where the data science and the service and experience design work together to curate and educate the AI to make the experience of interacting with it as effective as possible.

One of the design decisions at this stage has to do with carefully selecting from all the available data how much, and which parts, are going to be used to train the algorithm, and how much is going to be kept secret (untouched and unseen, a critical point) from the algorithm to test it later. The testing data needs to be as representative as the training data. Also, the amount of test data needs to be carefully selected. In the past, the rule of thumb has been to leave 20 percent of the whole dataset unseen to the algorithm, while using 80 percent as training data. Some modern deep learning approaches can use up to 99 percent of the data for training.

Now we can elaborate on the team composition and the role of testing. Training the AI and ML components is part of the data-science role that the team must engage in. They need to check the results of the algorithm when fed testing data that it has never seen before. One of the common pitfalls a team wants to avoid is using the same dataset to train and then test the algorithm. This will lead to the algorithm responding with great levels of accuracy for data it has seen during the training phase. A team that has fallen into this pitfall will be tempted to say that the ML component has reached a level of confidence that makes it deployable. The problem comes when faced with unknown data, making the output totally uncertain. There are many ways in which the test data can leak into the training set, which could be as simple as reckless repeated testing.

Finally, the team has to perform an evaluation of the algorithm in terms of sensitivity and cost. An error-free model does not exist, and not all errors are born alike. A false-positive (saying something is what it is not) is not the same as a false-negative (failing to say what something is). Think of it as misdiagnosing an illness (false-positive) against failing to tell you that you have the flu (false-negative). Some cases are critical (serious illnesses), so a higher rate of false-positive might be more acceptable. This can be taken to the extreme, however, such as flagging everyone as terrorists at an airport just to avoid missing one. On another, more retail-oriented example, over-forecasting might give us some working capital costs, while under-forecasting might cause lost sales to a competitor.

That trade-off is what is called a precision-recall trade-off, which needs to be tuned very specifically for each problem.

But how much training is enough? Is the AI just memorizing the data or extracting generalities from it? Is it just general enough to handle new data, or is it so general that it does not tell me anything nontrivial? The equilibrium between the overfitting (memorization) and generalization is another difficult alchemy to perform. A basic schematic of this concept for a simple classifier can be seen in figure 7.1.

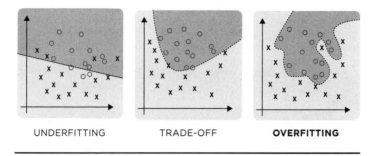

UNDERFITTING   TRADE-OFF   **OVERFITTING**

FIGURE 7.1: *Underfitting, overfitting, and a middle-ground trade-off on a classification example*

Throughout all this process, a core concern remains lurking below the surface. How am I measuring success, cost, preference? Is it aligned with business requirements? Is it technically helpful? How can I combine them? All metrics have biases and blind spots, and not all of them are mathematically useful for training!

Once the team is confident with the solution, it can work on converting the outcomes of the algorithms into insights, action items, predictions, or simply put: **Data Products**. The overall process can be seen, simplified, in figure 7.2.

The process is not quite finished at this point. Making sure that the trained algorithm, app, or system can actually work in production, scale, and be kept in control requires some heavy engineering skills. Through the monitoring of its behavior and use, feedback can be incorporated back into the problem definition and all the other stages. In fact, we can see in figure 7.3 a more truthful representation of the actual workflow, considering all the ways we can loop back to an earlier stage before moving forward.

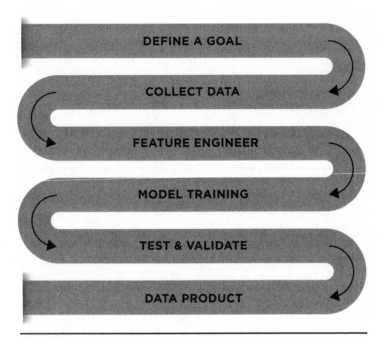

FIGURE 7.2: *Simplified AI process*

To wrap up, here are some key takeaways:

- The process of building an AI/ML component is more complex than just grabbing the data and trying out a few known algorithms with some existing libraries. Most likely, if you try to tackle an AI challenge this way, you will fall into the "Garbage in, Garbage out" pitfall.
- The process is far from linear. The team will probably loop back often, jumping from one stage to the other, in a way that might seem chaotic, which is likely to happen if not properly managed.

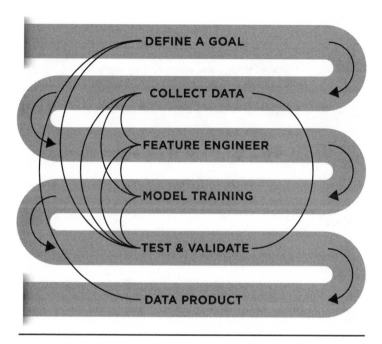

FIGURE 7.3: *A more realistic AI process*

- The jumps just mentioned are not necessarily in a cascade-esque fashion.
- To give appropriate visibility, the team needs to define measurable progress at the beginning of each sprint. Also, it's important to always align what the team is doing with business needs, and clearly communicate and commit to process transparency for the client stakeholders.
- The stages can be defined as: definition, collection and processing, training, validation and testing, deployment and monitoring.

CHAPTER 8
What an AI Project is Not

We will now take a look at the flip side and explore what an AI project is *not*—and discuss the warning signs that come when it is about to go off the rails.

NATURALLY AGILE

Agile" is a tricky concept to nail down in a context where everyone claims to be adopting it but at the same time trying to follow very strict processes and steps derived from a specific methodology.

We will reiterate the principles of the *agile manifesto* to clarify our preferred methodology:

- Individuals and interactions over processes and tools.
- Working software over comprehensive documentation.
- Customer collaboration over contract negotiation.
- Responding to change over following a plan.

For our purposes, adhering to an agile methodology is preferable when developing AI products. Things can get mixed up when teams introduce frameworks such as Scrum (a management and control process) or Kanban (a lean method to manage and improve work) in a zealous way to treat the complex mixture of research and development required for machine learning and the like.

A methodology is very much desired, as it gives structure, visibility, and order. In fact, the process we described in Chapter 7 can be easily subsumed under a methodology like CRISP-DM (data mining process model). The trick lies in the kinds of commitments we make and how we define the tasks. Experience tells us that we can commit more to different stages of an analytic strategy than what we can commit in terms of the accuracy/performance level of the task. Every analysis and experiment (training is defined as an experiment) has some underlying hypothesis that we seek to validate or reject. Having them as an explicit formulation and keeping track of the lessons learned enables us to advance in the strategy in a controlled way.

We still care about the raw performance of the AI, but the way to get there is the development of the project, not the result of a user story.

Having said that, many AI researchers and developers would object to the undignifying constraints and whims of a framework, accustomed to open-ended exploration rather than continuous tight deadlines. Still, those deadlines give structure and discipline, and for seasoned developers, add a lot of value.

Merging AI with agile is a road worth taking, but a path forged as you go.

JUST APIs

Using a scalpel does not make one a surgeon any more than consuming a cognitive API makes one an artificial intelligence developer. Insisting otherwise will make you a butcher, and not in a crafty way! Many IT workers of the past grumbled about the "script kiddies," who just used some templates and ready-made scripts without any understanding or control of what they were doing, yet dubbed themselves experts. The situation is much the same nowadays.

With the huge availability of resources, which we'll discuss in Chapter 9, it's easier than ever to start playing with this technology. And that is a good thing. But it is important to understand that "doing AI" involves the process, the care for the data and outcomes, and the integration and scalability we described.

If it can be described as "just using an API," then it's most likely not "doing AI."

PURE CHAOS

The process is heavily iterative, and the loops can begin or end at any stage. Described in Chapter 7, the process (page 88) is essentially a big loop comprising several smaller ones, a fractal of sorts.

But that does not translate to "out of control." The process still has a discipline to it; it still has tasks or stories of which we know the value up front; it can still be tracked. True, it might not fit perfectly within an agile framework, but that does not mean it's unruly.

There are projects that end up that way though. The most common ways to get there are through ill-defined aspects: the problem assessment, the relationship with the client, or the management.

An ill-defined problem is one where we are not sure what we are trying to achieve, but rather want to "add intelligence to something," and where the success criteria are akin to "we'll know when we get there." Expecting to be amazed just because you are calling it AI does not work. Not having a problem to solve does not work. Not knowing what value you are trying to deliver does not work.

An ill-defined relationship means that there is not enough trust in the capacity, whether technical or product, to allow for experimentation. It can also be micromanagement that pushes the team toward overcommitting, making promises that cannot be kept. AI projects always have a research bent; thus, they cannot be constrained to a pure "development hours" mind-set. Commitments need to be made and met, and trust must be earned, but through collaboration, not just control. Whether this relates to an external client or the governance team within the project, the outcome is the same. Without trust and commitment, no meaningful advances will be made.

PART IV

TOOLS

OVERVIEW
Tools

The rise of AI has been driven by the growing availability of new tools and services. They range from highly specific services to perform AI-related tasks to trained services, high-level data helpers, frameworks, and tools to build them. There are obvious trade-offs when it comes to either building your own AI components or using widely available ones. On the one hand, utilizing ready-made services means shortened time-to-market and generality of the task, while custom builds mean depth of control, extensibility, ownership, and value offering differential. It is also important to understand prevalent algorithms' NN architectures.

CHAPTER 9
AI Toolset Landscape

Throughout this section, which pertains to tools, we touch lightly upon the technical aspects, since we need to understand the basics behind the tools available, when and why to use them, and what considerations to keep in mind. Worst-case scenario: It suffices to simply familiarize yourself with the buzzwords that will surely be thrown around on an AI project!

On top of what we've been discussing, you may have heard of cognitive services, frameworks, languages . . . This chapter is about understanding the landscape of technologies and services in the market, and not getting overwhelmed with weird terms in the meantime.

The following sections will introduce the hierarchies, or "stacks," in which the technologies can be grouped. So, let's get to know what tools are out there.

COGNITIVE SERVICES

On one extreme, you have tools like Microsoft Azure Cognitive Services, IBM Watson, Google Cloud Platform Cloud AI, and others. Those tools provide you with a kind of black box approach to AI. What they have in common is that in some way they provide machine learning services, with pretrained models for straight-out consumption, and a service to generate your own tailored models.

When we discussed the buzzwords in Chapter 1, we mentioned that while the term "cognitive" had a clear differentiator intent upon its inception, it has become associated with the top layer of sophistication in AI offerings.

IBM Watson, for instance (as a much talked-about example), comes packed with a bunch of services that are made available through Bluemix. The services range from a Conversation API (to help build chatbots), Speech to Text API, Natural Language Understanding API, Personality Insights, Visual Recognition, and more. Also, there is IBM Watson Machine Learning, which is a full-service Bluemix offering that makes it easy for developers and data scientists to work together to integrate predictive capabilities with their applications. The Machine Learning service is a set of REST APIs that can be called from any programming language to develop applications.

In the same way, Google GCP Cloud AI provides services that will perform general analysis on different types of input streams: video and image, audio (speech), and text analysis (Google Natural Language API). If these pretrained algorithms do not fit your needs, Google also has a Machine Learning Engine service, which will provide you with managed services that enable you to easily build machine learning models. Cloud Machine Learning Engine can take any TensorFlow model and perform large-scale training on a managed cluster.

Microsoft is another big player in this scene, providing the same type of services that IBM and Google are offering. Through Azure, they expose services to access pretrained algorithms, and in case you need a pinch more, you can tap into the Machine Learning services. Some offerings, such as conversational services, come in a whole array through LUIS.

SPECIFIC APIs

Then, in the middle of the spectrum there are the task-specific services and tools such as image recognition with the likes of Clarifai, conversational tools with Dialogflow (previously known as Api.ai), text processing with MonkeyLearn, and so on. Microsoft's LUIS framework could be thought of as a detached specific service if needed.

There are many more specific APIs than cognitive services, so we won't go too deep into naming and classifying them, but rather provide an overview of how they are offered and used.

These APIs represent already trained models that are ripe for consumption. You don't usually get much control over how they are trained or the specific objective they are seeking to solve, but on the other hand, there is no need to concern ourselves with that. If the intended purpose and subject matter suit our needs, we can just consume them as a service and integrate them into our applications and processes. It's on us to be sure that they are aligned with the subject matter, and not expect Clarifai to point out the kind of bone fracture presented in an X-ray unless trained to do so. These services are aimed at one particular type of task—and focus on being really good at it.

So far, we presented the layers that focus on the kind of *function* we want to exert—the *what* from this point on, we'll present tools that let us define *how* we want to achieve it.

BUILD TOOLS

On the other extreme, you have your good old friends like Python, R, and Matlab. Those tools have been around for several years and are the core of the basic survival kit for many data scientists. You can do traditional ML with those tools and programming languages. You could build your own deep neural network from scratch in Java, C++, C, or other languages—though today, apart from an educational endeavor, this would mean reinventing the wheel.

It is fair to point out that Python has gained a tremendous track record in the data community. In particular, libraries/frameworks like Pandas and scikit-learn are making a lot of progress on data analysis and ML.

Then deep learning showed up, and frameworks such as TensorFlow, PyTorch, Keras, Caffe, CNTK, MXNet, and Gluon appeared. These tools allow you to build deep neural networks, many natively in Python, some with their own lingo and some with community-driven APIs so they can be used on top of the programing language of choice.

At the time of this writing, TensorFlow and PyTorch are the ones getting the most traction and growth. TensorFlow is an open-source project by Google. Similarly, Torch is open source and was first created by Facebook in Lua, and the Python port, PyTorch, has an impressive amount of activity in their community.

There are also what we call "high-level helpers," which are tools where you still have to build your AI, but the process is made much simpler and easier. Bonsai, for example, built a domain-specific language (DSL) for AI, which looks like a mixture of SQL and Python, with the aim of giving the same level of abstraction and capabilities to AI that SQL gave to databases, where what gets modeled are the lessons rather than the architecture of a deep neural network. H20.ai, on the other hand, gives tools to make it easier to design, build, and train deep learning models, going so far as to claim they enable "driverless AI."

Last but not least, tools like Anaconda, Jupyter, and FloydHub help data scientists avoid doing the heavy lifting of software engineering tasks by themselves. For example, Anaconda is a fully integrated data science ecosystem, born from Python. Jupyter and Zeppelin are a simple way for data scientists to produce analysis and share reproducible code, while FloydHub is a "Heroku" kind of service designed to help with setting up and all the cumbersome tasks that no one likes to deal with (researchers and developers alike), such as setting up cloud environments, managing them and the experiments run on them, etc.

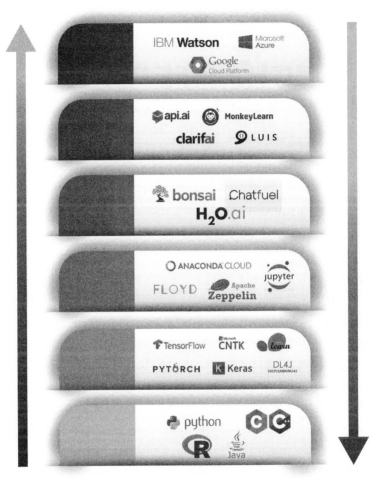

GENERALITY
AND IMMEDIACY

DEGREES OF
FREEDOM, OWNERSHIP

FIGURE 9.1: *Hierarchies in the tool landscape*

In summary, we can think of the offerings as a *sophistication vs. freedom* hierarchy, as illustrated in figure 9.1.

CHAPTER 10
Using Ready-Made AI
vs. Building Our Own

Now we know about these different services and the tools you can use to build your own AI from scratch, but you may be wondering, *What is the best option? How do I approach that decision?* These questions arise in some cases due to the misconception that AI is complete, solved, done, and that a single AI applies to everything. But AI is like a library; it does some things very well, and those parts are already done, but it's not the same for every scenario or need.

We have Watson, Azure, Amazon, Google, and others, and they have models, which are trained and ready for some specific tasks, and for general cases, they will work very well. But if we need to have more control or need more specific answers or tasks from them, then things might get a bit more complicated for those solutions.

TRADE-OFFS

The decision comes down to a set of trade-offs, which we need to solve.

What am I trying to accomplish? If the problem can be framed in a way that is broad enough, and the subject matter general enough, then there is a very good chance that there is already a service available for what I need. But I may want to explore a specific subject matter or give a different solution to the problem—or bring innovation or scale or some other thing to the table.

The capabilities at our disposal are of consequence, too. *Do I have the kind of talent required to build my own services? Do I at least have availability of resources that can understand and deal with these services? Or am I expecting to be a straight-up consumer without getting the team's feet in the mud?*

But it also depends on the stage of development of our initiative. It makes no sense to build a new Watson from scratch if we are only testing how a question analyzer would feel in our product, or redo Alexa just for the sake of testing voice commands. On the other hand, if we are headed for production and the AI component is core to our offering and the source of our differential value, we might not want to outsource just that.

Let's say we show a picture of an X-ray to Google photo AI. The AI might say it's an X-ray; it will not say that you have a fissure on a bone, as it was not trained to dive into that specific knowledge. We need to balance the specificity and generality and how much we want to control and own versus our openness to future changes.

In Chapter 9, we illustrated the hierarchy of AI offerings, where the higher we are, the more sophisticated the offering is, requiring less work while relinquishing degrees of control over the outcome and workings.

The amount of time needed to go to market is among the reasons to go higher in the hierarchy, as the AI component is ready-made. Along those same lines, less code or development is required, as it is a service that is already exposed for consumption. There is less need for training, or no training at all, depending on the tool and use case. This will imply a broader generality of the subject domain. At proof-of-concept and design phases, it's usually a sure bet to start near the top.

On the lower echelons, there is an increasing degree of control over the design and behavior of the AI, as the algorithm can be customized both in terms of the architecture and processes, as well as the specific domain knowledge, by controlling the kind of input data and labels used. Having full control of the solution enables more ownership over aspects of privacy and security. If we are looking to have a highly differentiated value offering in which the core is based on AI, then it's most likely that the effort to develop this deep pays off.

There is not a clear-cut use case to choose one or the other, but rather a set of considerations to ponder. The trade-offs need to be discussed with all involved parties, whether it be what can be committed for the budget, what the expected value and design is, what skills and capacities the developers are comfortable with, and so on. AI is always a team sport, and needs to be treated as such.

CHAPTER 11
Some Core Tools: Algorithms

The final step in understanding the tools of AI is going to its core: the machine learning algorithms that power all the rest of the chain. While this chapter does indeed get more technical than other chapters, we are still aiming to describe it in such a way that gives you an intuitive grasp over the algorithms rather than an operational, mathematical description.

The objective is to give you an idea of the capabilities of these building blocks and the different options available, as well as familiarize you with some of the terms you might hear in team discussions or offerings with core AI components.

To give context to what was presented in Chapter 9, when we are discussing the algorithms, we are talking about the lower levels of the hierarchy of offerings, namely, raw code and frameworks like TensorFlow and PyTorch, or even high-level helpers like H20.ai, where the user can build or select the algorithm of choice.

In the upper realms of that hierarchy, the user can only select a function they want to perform, being abstracted from the underlying mechanism at play.

At this stage, we'll focus on supervised learning algorithms given the explicit goal we are looking at and because they are the most developed and deployed, as discussed in Chapter 6. We can classify the tasks in two broad groups (among many others): classification and regression.

CLASSIFICATION

The objective of a classification algorithm is to assess or decide the membership of a new datum among some classes. This could be as simple as just one, like the now-infamous "Hot Dog or Not Hot Dog," from the TV show *Silicon Valley*, to as many as we can handle.

Naive Bayes

"Naive" in this case means that it expects or assumes things to be "simple," which in the case of an algorithm, would mean that the different factors are not interrelated. So, naive Bayes classifiers identify the probability that each factor has in making an element a member of each class.

If we go back to our *Go_to_the_beach* predictive model (see page 74), it will try to assess the probability of *Go_to_the_beach* as the result of the joint conditional probability of just *Go_to_the_beach* considered as a random variable, *Outlook* given the case where *Go_to_the_beach* were true, and the same with *Temperature* and *Humidity*, all mediated by the evidence we have of the case.

Yes, it sounds complicated, and as with almost everything Bayesian in nature, it normally is, unless we get very deep in technical terms.

Let's just say that it considers the probability of each factor independently, conditional to the case we are assessing and the evidence we have (the sample we take), with a strong assumption that the factors and their effects are independent.

It has very nice statistical properties, and scales very well compared to other traditional machine learning algorithms.

Support Vector Machines

Other classification algorithms are support vector machines (SVM). They try to find a hyperplane that separates the two classes with as much distance as possible from the data points to the boundary.

Hyper-what? When we have only two variables, we can use a graph with the x-axis being one of them, for example, *Temperature* in our *Go_to_the_beach* example and *Humidity* on the y-axis. We might be able to find a straight line in that case. If we add another variable, *Outlook*, then a line is not going to cut it anymore, and we'll need a plane. What happens when we keep adding variables? We still seek to find a "straight" division boundary in whatever number of dimensions—features—we have. The mathematical term describing that is the hyperplane.

The boundary is mathematically represented as a vector, on which the machine relies to classify, hence the name.

It can be extended in many ways, like multiclass classifications problems through the "one vs. all" mechanic, or generate "infinite dimensions" through the kernel trick, in a way that will make the boundary seem "not straight" in the original dimensions.

It is a very powerful classical algorithm, oftentimes used as a benchmark, but one which does not scale so well into production.

k-Nearest Neighbors

KNN could be seen as the laziest algorithm of them all. The easiest way to think about it is "guilt by association"—if you are surrounded by guilty people, chances are you are also involved.

We choose a number of nearby data points to the one we are assessing, k, and we decide that the class of k is the same as its neighbors'. That's it!

And it still works beautifully. But selecting the value of k is not trivial, and scaling this up to be used in production can be problematic, while also giving us no clues about the *why*.

Decision Trees

A decision tree is a hugely popular predictive modeling approach to machine learning algorithms for classifications. They seek to build a stack of *if-then* decisions that will end up defining the class of the data point. It's called a tree in the same way a family tree graphs.

There are different ways in which these rules are constructed (with as much variety as is seen in species of trees), but the essence of the mechanics is that they seek, for every variable, how much information is gained in classifying the samples if we set up a decision boundary.

Let's say that on our *Go_to_the_beach* predictive model

(see page 74), considered all together, there are 30 percent of instances where *Go_to_the_beach* is true and 70 percent where it is false. If we divide the data by *Temperature, high* on one side and *low* on the other, we have a different situation. On the *Temperature = High* batch, *Go_to_the_beach* is true on 80 percent of the cases, and when *Temperature = Low*, *Go_to_the_beach* is true on only 2 percent of the cases.

We gained quite a lot of information from that division! Still, we need to evaluate the other variables, the hierarchy, how they chain together, if the percentage of true cases is the appropriate measure, what happens if we have temperature in degrees rather than a class, and so on.

Decision trees are very powerful, can be used successfully in production, give us the decision order and the boundaries . . . all very cool benefits, which explain their popularity. They have many subtleties on how to avoid overfitting and generalization, while keeping the explanatory value, but let's leave that to the practitioners of the craft.

REGRESSION

The name *regression* has a historical context, which is very interesting but out of the scope of this text. Suffice it to say that it has come to simply mean "value estimators"— that is, instead of saying whether *Temperature* will fall under the class "high" or "low," we are interested in knowing *how many degrees Celsius* will it be.

Generalized Regression

This family of algorithms comes from the field of statistics and has a very strong foundation in theory and application, although that also means there are conditions that have to be met (some more restrictive than others) to be sure that the technique actually leverages that foundation and is in control.

The first in the family of algorithms developed was the linear regression, where a straight line is fitted to the data points on the case of a single value used as independent variable. It is linear in the sense that the relationship between the target and the input follows the linear function $Y = a + bX$.

It may not be as easy to "see" the straight line with multiple independent variables, but the functional form stays the same.

A huge benefit of this approach is the possibility of identifying the individual contribution of each factor, a bunch of statistics to assess if they are significant, and so on. If one of my X factors increases by one, I know exactly how much different the output will be.

The family of statistical methods extends to logistic regression, where the target value, the outcome, is a value between zero and one, oftentimes interpreted as a probability. A sigmoid function (hence the "logistic" part) is composed by the linear regression mentioned earlier, resulting in a nonlinear function.

If we define the outcome of the logistic regression as the probability of belonging to a class, then we can use this as a classification algorithm, coupled with some sort of threshold or comparison rule.

Even more generality can be found within the generalized linear model, where, in the same way that we used the logistic function, we can use many link functions so that we are "regressing" towards several statistical functions, such as the identity link (linear regression), the logit link (logistic regression), logarithm (log-regression for Poisson distributions), and so on.

Regression Tree

What if we want to use the power of decision trees but to output a real-valued number instead of a class? Then we have regression trees, which build upon both regression and decision trees, while keeping many of the good qualities of both.

Although we will not get into the implementation details, a rough way of understanding regression trees is if you imagine dividing the target variable into many small chunks, sort of nano-classes, where the value of the target variable is the mean of that class.

Time Series Models

When we are looking at the change of a given variable through time, we are looking at a time series. There are many different approaches to deal with them, whether utilizing regression or more specialized methods, such as ARIMA, state-space models, and so on. The underlying idea is to use past values to estimate future values of the same variable.

Time series are usually of interest when making a decision

about a future event but when the actual cause is not of interest. For many economic applications, the properties of the model (like ARIMA and derivations) are of interest, even more so than the output value.

When dealing with time series models, the pragmatic objective of having the target value is usually preferred to the exact logic of why that value is the one.

NEURAL NETWORKS

We need to break down our categories (regression and classification) when we talk about neural networks in general, which provide several different architectures to accomplish both of those tasks.

We'll describe the different broad families to get an understanding of the kinds of tasks they can accomplish.

Deep NNs

Deep neural networks are the general family of algorithms, which were discussed in previous chapters. The basic characteristic is the capacity to have several layers of depth (or many computational graph nodes between input and output for non-layered architectures), through which they can learn complex representations of the input variables.

Convolutional NNs

A convolutional neural network is one where there are specific layers that act as "convolution filters." Simple, right?

Let's review its essential premise.

Convolutional networks were inspired by biological processes, more specifically by the organization of the animal visual cortex. Individual neurons respond to stimuli only in a restricted region of the visual field known as the receptive field. The receptive fields of different neurons partially overlap such that they cover the entire visual field (i.e., some neurons in the visual region only fire up when they "see" vertical stripes).

Mathematically, a convolution (like the name suggests) is a complex operation between functions, which outputs another one. In the visual cortex case, one function is the "visual stimuli" and the other one is the "neural receptivity" for a given region. The output, the third function, is all the kinds of signals that could be sent from that interaction. You can imagine the convolution as a small sliding window moving through an image and fully covering it.

It is a way to specify beforehand to the NN that the "spatial structure" of the input has a meaning, making it much easier to learn it.

In the CNN architecture, a convolutional layer applies a convolution operation to the input, passing the result to the next layer. This convolution operation allows the network to be deeper with much less parameters, which makes them a viable and practical solution to image processing.

CNNs give huge improvements even when using relatively little preprocessing compared to other image classification algorithms. This means that the network learns the filters (the operation that the sliding window applies) that in traditional algorithms were hand-engineered. This independence from prior knowledge and human effort in feature design is a major advantage.

The key point of CNNs is that they leverage the prior knowledge that there might be a spatial relationship in the input to that layer (pixels in image, placement of words in a phrase, etc.) to be learned. So, it just needs to learn how, and not if.

RECURRENT NNS

What if the prior knowledge that I want to leverage is not of a spatial (or concurrent) relationship, but rather that the input represents a sequence of sorts?

Humans don't start their thinking from scratch every second. As you read a book, for example, you understand each word based on your understanding of previous words. You don't throw everything away and start thinking from scratch again. Your thoughts have persistence, memory.

Out of the box, neural networks simply can't do this. For example, imagine you want to classify what kind of event is happening at every point in a movie. It's unclear how a neural network could use its reasoning about previous events in the film to inform later ones, unless you input "the whole movie" as input, every time.

Recurrent neural networks (RNN) address this issue. They are networks with memory loops in them, allowing information to persist. This means that the output depends not only on the current input, but on the state of the neuron, representing past inputs.

Long Short-Term Memory

RNNs have many difficulties in training, remembering long-term relationships, stability, and so on. That made the practical applications of them . . . underwhelming.

Long short-term memory networks (LSTM) are a special kind of RNN, capable of learning long-term dependencies, thereby making it possible to use RNNs at scale!

LSTMs are explicitly designed to avoid the long-term dependency problem. The key to them is that they "learn" what/when to remember (their "state") and what to forget.

In the last few years, there has been incredible success applying RNNs to a variety of problems: speech recognition, language modeling, translation and image captioning.

GENERATIVE ADVERSARIAL NETWORKS

The latest developments in the world of neural networks is a different way to approach the training process and architecture.

We know that we can use a DNN to classify data. We know that we can use DNNs to generate new data. What would happen if we make them compete with each other?

Generative adversarial networks (GAN) do just that. They pit a generative network creating instances of data (text, image, sound, or any other) that tries to pass them off as legitimate, real-world data against a network whose job it is to discriminate the real samples from the generated ones.

If trained correctly (which is harder than with every other DNN), at some point the discriminator gets lost, being unable to distinguish real from fake samples, not through some vice in the training but due to the quality of the fake data. At that point, we have a mechanism to generate data that is indistinguishable from real-world data!

This has been used a lot for generating new images, music, texts, and so on, but it has also led to huge improvements in semi-supervised learning. This means that we have some labeled samples, but not enough, so we can try to generate more samples to learn better.

The workings of the arrangement are quite complex, but let's just say that this technique can improve the results over small samples by orders of magnitude.

Ensemble

Ensemble learning is the strategy of combining many different models into one productive unit. This approach revolves around the idea of voting, or arbitration, in some way.

The beauty of ensemble learning is that different models can be used on the same dataset, assign different weights to the output of each model, and then poll all the models (taking into consideration their weight) to choose the output with more votes.

This usually leads to models that generalize better, predict better, and that are more stable, though less likely to anticipate black swans.

In fact, neural networks can be described as an ensemble of ensembles, with each layer representing one kind of ensemble, and the whole architecture the other.

In fact, CNNs and RNNs work as such, with layers of different kinds serving different purposes.

There are many ways to use these ensembles. It could be set to use case-specific algorithms for some pieces of data, voting across all the algorithms (like in random forests), weighting the outputs of the different algorithms to produce a new one, or even having the resolution mechanic as one more aspect of the algorithm to be learned.

PART V
AI AT WORK

OVERVIEW
AI at Work

There are myriad applications of AI in relation to various types of businesses. It's important to explore and seek out additional applications to become comfortable with what's possible. There are also numerous nontechnical aspects of AI, such as cultural biases, regulations, and creativity, which need to be considered and understood as industries explore potential applications. The power of AI has also led to fear and concern over their potential impact on our lives. Distinguishing between fact and fiction is a necessary part of the journey, and as AI becomes more ingrained in all aspects of our businesses and individual lives, the dialogue will become increasingly important.

CHAPTER 12
Sample Applications and Projects

We will now discuss several examples of how AI has been used to provide value, what techniques can be used, and what companies are doing—and try to present them by use case and not by business or vertical.

USE CASE VS. BUSINESS VERTICALS

There is a reason to avoid "verticals," which can be summed up as follows:

- **Cross-pollination:** Regardless of where something is being done and who is doing it, a great source of innovation comes from taking those deeds and applying them to a new context. What would happen if you try to do the cases we describe in your business?

- **State-of-the-art techniques:** AI is changing the way we do things across the board, and that is not defined by business. It may enable us to do things we were unable to do before, however.

- **Job description:** Creativity and innovation are still a necessary focus in our jobs, whether in business models or the technologies we use. Verticals can act as limiting anchors.

The objective in discussing the following cases is to feature cross-pollination and to inspire and give an overall sense of the possibilities. These examples are not meant to be limiting—the next killer app is just around the corner!

RECOMMENDER SYSTEMS
NETFLIX AND OTHER FORMS OF MEDIA

Netflix has a very famous recommendation engine. It even has a famous contest for teams trying to improve upon it.

The content suggestions are influenced by the kinds of things a user has watched and the popularity of a particular title, among other variables. Over 75 percent of what people watch comes from Netflix's recommendation engine.[1]

AMAZON.COM

The retail industry is more dynamic than ever. Amazon has implemented a very powerful recommendation engine, which makes on-site recommendations (such as the "recommended for you" or the "frequently bought together" sections) and off-site suggestions (via email) based on your purchase history, the history from similar users, and the products' characteristics.

The results are impressive, with over 35 percent of Amazon's revenue being generated by its recommendation engine.[2]

1. Xavier Amatriain and Justin Basilico, "Netflix Recommendations: Beyond the 5 stars (Part 1)," *Netflix Technology Blog* (April 5, 2012), medium.com/netflix-techblog/netflix-recommendations-beyond-the-5-stars-part-1-55838468f429.
2. Ian Mackenzie, Chris Meyer, and Steve Noble, "How retailers can keep up with consumers," McKinsey & Company (October 2013), www.mckinsey.com/industries/retail/our-insights/how-retailers-can-keep-up-with-consumers.

ASSISTANTS & CHATBOTS

ALEXA, SIRI, GOOGLE HOME . . .

All these systems use speech recognition, natural language understanding, and speech generation in order to understand what users are asking for, and act on it.

The good thing about these systems is that they store every interaction that users make and then use that data to train and improve algorithms.

Did we say good? We also meant *scary*!

Q&A

Several companies are integrating new communication channels with their customers, using chatbots. These bots are empowered by NLU techniques, so they can understand intentions, entities, and even the mood behind the text the users write, and then respond with the best answer.

AI models with memory give chatbots the ability to remember the context and to create meaningful and frictionless conversations.

TUTORING

Chatbots are not always used to give a particular answer to a particular question. They can also be conversational companions that guide instead of providing ready-made solutions.

This is particularly valuable in education, but also any time where assistance does not have a definite answer.

SEAMLESS SHOPPING USER EXPERIENCE
Amazon Go

AI is also changing how we interact with the brick-and-mortar world. Amazon Go is an example of it.

Amazon's engineers are trying to create a completely seamless shopping experience . . . a brick-and-mortar retail store where you can enter, grab some items, and leave without any interaction with cashiers, receiving the billing in your Amazon account after the transaction.

PROCESS OPTIMIZATION
Amazon Fresh

Amazon Fresh allows customers to combine grocery and other shopping into a seamless experience. They use AI techniques to determine which products are fresh, and which are not, so they can send the better products to their clients.

By using AI, the company can learn from the best masters and connoisseurs and scale that knowledge far away from what a single person or team can do, while keeping the quality standard.

Search Prediction

You may have noticed that when you type some characters on Google's search bar, the auto-complete suggestions are very, very accurate. It looks like Google knows us better than we know ourselves or that someone is reading our minds—except when they're not and it gets very weird or funny . . .

This search prediction uses your history, your location, your profile, and information coming from other users, to identify and recommend what you're looking for.

Ad Placing

When you visit a site and you see advertising that suspiciously fits your needs or your plans, and is exactly what you were looking for . . . well, you know that AI algorithms were running in the background.

Content or advertising customization is an interesting application of collaborative filtering, and it is also trained with the result of millions of A/B tests on advertising campaigns.

FinTech

There are actually a lot of AI-powered applications in the fintech (financial services) world. Some examples are fraud detection and prevention, stock value forecasting, and valuation modeling using sentiment analysis and topic extraction.

Calls Transcripts

Call centers have hundreds of thousands of recorded calls. Using speech recognition, we can process these audio files and convert them into a structured knowledge base.

By adding topic extraction or sentiment analysis capabilities, we can deeply analyze and tag this content and extract valuable information from it.

INVENTORY LEVELS

Image recognition can be used in various applications. The use of object recognition can give a system the capability of counting items in a shell or deposit and trigger actions if some level is decaying, which will enable us to automatically manage inventory levels, based just on camera views, eliminating the need to rely on reports.

REVENUE OPTIMIZATION

PRICING

Many online retail stores are dynamically setting the price of their wares using machine learning algorithms that estimate the price for an item based on users and their context, with the goal of maximizing sales or revenue.

ATTRITION PREDICTION

Every user-based business is worried about the attrition rate. The problem with attrition is that a company can only be aware of it after the user is already gone.

What if we can predict in advance when a user is going to leave? What if we can identify the specific reasons to trigger recovery action? Or understand what we need to improve to avoid people leaving?

A lot of e-learning platforms, for example, are implementing attrition prediction to know if a user is going to drop a course and tackle the reasons for that behavior before the user actually leaves.

WELLNESS

SENIOR HEALTHCARE

There are some joint initiatives between AI and IoT to improve the life quality of elder people. Algorithms are being trained to detect, and even predict, the occurrence of a home accident or a health breakdown, so doctors and families can be aware of the situation and react faster. This could actually save lives.

ALTERED EMOTIONAL & COGNITIVE STATES

Using AI, it is possible to detect facial expressions and voice prosody to determine the emotional state of a person. Having this knowledge can lead to the creation of even more adaptive and customized digital journeys for users that fit not only their needs but how are they feeling at any given moment.

CHAPTER 13
Rounding It Up

There are many sides to AI beyond technique, such as bias, regulation, creativity, and so on. We'll review them here, plus give you some references to keep learning on your own.

SMALL RECAPITULATION

We have talked about terminology and key concepts of AI to give you the framework with which to participate in the dialogue. We discussed the conditions under which AI and ML can be applied and which tools can be used for different challenges, providing the proper tools and mind-set to ask the right questions and identify opportunities.

Finally, we explored some real-world applications of AI and ML. Combined with all the rest, we hope to have awakened the inner AI Padawan that lies within you. If we did and you want to keep on digging deeper, here is a list of resources with which to investigate, as well as experts to follow and online training opportunities (and heads up: More ML and DL trainings will be forthcoming).

This chapter is not as clear-cut as previous ones, since we need to step away from the realm of pure technology. Artificial intelligence is powerful enough that we cannot avoid its philosophical aspects. It has such an impact on the world, we need to examine these aspects.

BIASES

Sexism, racism, xenophobia, and every other kind of bias that exists in society is unavoidably present in artificial intelligence.

Some might remember the case of the HP[1] computer vision software that aimed to track a person's face and follow the movements with the webcam. That worked pretty well for a young, Caucasian female, but it did not work on a young African-American male, perhaps due to some cameras having issues with contrast recognition in certain lighting situations. Something similar happened to Google[2] back in 2015 when a photo of an African-American family was AI tagged as "gorillas" (or shrewdness of apes).

Were the algorithms racist? Were those examples a bug? The answer is in fact pretty straightforward: They learned what they were taught. The training dataset selected to tackle those problems did not contemplate or did not have enough examples of African-Americans, so the algorithms were not tweaked correctly, hence, the classification error.

Another case is a groundbreaking study on why chatbots tend to be sexist. They found that the bulk of the data used for

1. Mallory Simon, "HP looking into claim webcams can't see black people," *CNN* (December 23, 2009), www.cnn.com/2009/TECH/12/22/hp.webcams/index.html.
2. See page 90.

training had words like "women" and "girl" in the contexts of "house," "family," and "mother," while "boy" and "man" were used in contexts of "work," "success," and the like.

The issue is *lack of data science* and *too much focus on algorithms*, since the foundational dataset was working with unchecked biases, so expecting the bot to not learn them was naive at best.

Another consideration is how to build the systems in a way that avoids reinforcing social inequalities. As Cathy O'Neil describes in her book *Weapons of Math Destruction*, algorithms and big data can (and do) perpetuate inequalities, which, instead of improving society, have a serious deleterious effect.[3]

How can that happen? When the models used are opaque (not transparent), unregulated, without the proper feedback mechanisms, and executed on a massive scale, they can generate and reinforce ecosystems of inequalities. For example, in the United States, if a low-income student can't get a loan because a lending model deems him too risky (by virtue of his zip code), he's then cut off from the kind of education that could pull him out of poverty, resulting in a vicious cycle.

REGULATION AND POLICIES

This little mathematical "thing," the AI, is going to be making decisions. When those fail or have negative consequences, who is going to be responsible?

We are very accustomed to organizing ourselves around a responsibility principle—*someone* is responsible for the

3. Cathy O'Neil, *Weapons of Math Destruction: How Big Data Increases Inequality and Threatens Democracy*, New York: Broadway Books, September 6, 2016.

decisions and consequences of actions. When things run afoul, who should be held accountable? The people who trained the AI, the ones who used it, the data providers, the regulators . . .?

The question is how and when to regulate it. Is regulation going to decide what kind of data we can use to build an AI, thus imposing a limit to its potential from the start? Is it going to affect the final decision, overriding AI for some specific cases, akin to affirmative-discrimination practices, enforcing a preferred bias of its own? Or maybe it will affect the outcome of a certain population, for instance, forbidding the denial of loans to more than X percent of applicants from a disadvantaged group? What about prioritization in healthcare or education?

The thorny issue, in the end, is that you cannot regulate ethics into the AI, nor can you avoid the subsequent decisions—AI will just learn from what it has been given as an example. The famous "trolley problem" (an ethics dilemma in which you must decide if would you kill one person to save five) is as relevant as ever—and even more so with autonomous cars and the like.

As AI grows into more and more areas, those implied decisions will begin to shape our world, and we need to be aware of the kind of moral behaviors we engineer into them.

CREATIVITY AND AI

It's not all doom and gloom, however. On the positive side, we can explore the creative frontiers of AI development.

In recent months, start-ups and some individuals moved

from investigation and research of deep neural networks applied to signal processing (sound, images, and text) to other sorts of jaw-dropping and dazzling applications. Style transferring with deep learning, for example, recomposes an image in the look and feel of another image by using a stream of data as input to apply a certain style to that input to generate an output. So, for example, the input could be an image and the style could be the patterns of Edvard Munch's painting *The Scream*. The output will be the original image with the look and feel of *The Scream*.

Another example is text generation using a particular writer's style. Let's say you train a model with the whole Shakespeare bibliography and then give some input stimuli to the model; it generates an output text with Shakespeare's writing style. Pretty awesome, right?

Last but not least, Aiva Technologies claims to be an artificial intelligence that composes emotional soundtrack music. The approach is a bit different from style transfer, but the whole concept is similar: train models with classical (or other genre) music, and given a certain input stimuli, generate music that follows the pattern the algorithm has been trained with.

This, of course, begs the question, can AI be creative? Does it even make sense to question whether AI is creative? What does it mean to have creativity? What is art? Can a machine create art?

We consider AI technologies as very elaborate and sophisticated tools for expressing creativity—tools with a potential never seen before in humankind.

FURTHER STUDIES

If you are interested in keeping up with developments in AI and studying a bit on your own, there are a couple of resources you can use. This is in no way an exhaustive list, but rather a curated starting point.

Andrew Ng is well known in AI circles. He has his own blog that is highly recommended. His twitter account is very interesting. His Machine Learning course is one of the best on Coursera, which, by the way, he cofounded. He was involved in the rise of Google as an AI powerhouse, as well as Baidu.

The Baidu AI research blog is an interesting source of material. Additionally, the DeepMind site is a great place to look for interesting advances in AI.

Yann LeCun is an all-around deep learning expert, the inventor of the convolutional neural networks, and head of AI research at Facebook—a top technical guy!

Andrej Karpathy is the director of AI intelligence at Tesla, and lectures on some of the best technical lessons about deep learning. Look him up on YouTube.

Coursera and Udacity both have great courses on machine learning, AI, NLP, data science, self-driving cars, and so on. Beware of going to the deep learning courses before taking the introductory courses on machine learning or even data science, as it can become a very steep obstacle.

There are many more resources to check out, and you can follow the links from these starting points to explore your interests.

CHAPTER 14
The Dark Side

While we are very excited about AI, we have to acknowledge it has a potential dark side. What are we really talking about when we mention the dangers of AI?

UNKNOWN UNKNOWNS

The first thing to point out is that we are not discussing a Terminator or Skynet scenario. It's not because it's not dangerous to use AI to make some sort of autonomous military equipment, but rather because we are still very far away from that potential, and other dangers are more insidious.

In an evolutionary sense, we are creating what is potentially an entity that can compete with us for resources within our own environments. And we are creating it to outperform us in any task that we can think of.

The danger then is to get displaced—"Darwin'ed," if you like—by an entity that can learn faster than us and adapt faster than us, but one requiring the same resources that we need to survive.

We don't need to reach a singularity scenario—or the point at which all the advances in technology will lead to machines that are smarter than people—for this to happen. The entity does not need consciousness, whether you think of it as a virus, a protozoan life-form, or something akin to Dawkins's "selfish gene."

What actually happens in those cases is that the comprehension of this AI-created entity is too narrow to understand concepts such as sustaining the environment in which it operates. Humans don't seem to be doing very well on this front either. Can we teach it in that case?

Given that, we can focus on *when* AI will become dangerous, and that is when we have ill-advised objectives with unforeseeable consequences.

What if an AI determines that for some production value it should modify the climate, without human habitability being part of that equation, or calculating the value of our loved ones by a strict utilitarian or economic value.

This type of creation can be extremely efficient, but without the capacity to have a sense of *why*, how is this efficiency useful? The danger is that the action comes without the thinking. Is it about intelligence versus wisdom?

LA RESISTANCE

There are very bright minds that are up to the challenge, warning about and trying to find a way to keep AI in control. The potential danger is not a deal-breaker, but rather a wake-up call, reminding us that we need some serious science on how this thing evolves and how it is controlled, coupled with serious philosophical work about what it means to be smart, to have sense, to have an objective that is coherent with the existence of other living beings.

In the end, AI is dangerous because you can't engineer a meaning to existence. We still need to define it, even before we try to find a way to imbue AI with it.

EPILOGUE

This book is meant to be an overview, a way to avoid getting lost when discussing AI. There is an endless sea of information you can discover: research, developments, businesses, and start-ups.

AI is a reality now. The sooner we get on board, the better. You don't need a PhD to start playing with AI. You just need to get your hands dirty. AI is a team effort. It's not about a specific technical background, but about being part of it. It's about embracing AI to achieve augmented intelligence.

—The Globant AI Team

DISCLAIMER

APPENDICES

GLOSSARY
Terms & Definitions

AGILE SOFTWARE DEVELOPMENT: A set of
fundamental principles about how software should be
developed based on an agile way of working, in contrast
to previous heavy-handed software development
methodologies.

ALGORITHM: A step-by-step procedure designed to
perform an operation, or formula for solving a problem,
based on conducting a sequence of specified actions.

ARTIFICIAL INTELLIGENCE: Artificial intelligence is
the idea that machines can be built with an intelligence
comparable to that of a human.

ARTIFICIAL GENERAL INTELLIGENCE (AGI): AI that
is not purposely built for a narrowly defined task, but rather
to be able to do many things in a similar way a human
would.

ARTIFICIAL NARROW INTELLIGENCE: AI that is
focused on one narrow task; for example, computer vision,
speech processing, music generation (or sound generation
in a more general way), and playing games such as poker.

ARTIFICIAL NEURAL NETWORK (ANN): Artificial neural networks, or connectionist systems, are computing systems inspired by the biological neural networks that constitute animal brains. Such systems learn (progressively improve performance on) tasks by considering examples, generally without task-specific programming.

CHATBOTS: A computer program that conducts a conversation via auditory or textual methods.

CLOUD COMPUTING: Rather than using a local server or a personal computer, cloud computing utilizes a network of remote servers hosted on the Internet to store, manage, and process data.

COGNITIVE SERVICES: A set of APIs, SDKs, and ready-made services and models designed for developers to make their applications more intelligent, engaging, and discoverable.

CONVOLUTIONAL NEURAL NETWORK (CNN or ConvNet): In machine learning, a convolutional neural network is a class of deep, feed-forward artificial neural networks that have successfully been applied to analyzing visual imagery.

DATA ARCHITECTURE: This refers to a set of rules, policies, standards, and models that define and dictate the type of data collected and how it is used, stored, managed, and integrated within an organization and its database systems.

DATA SCIENCE: Also known as data-driven science, this is an interdisciplinary field about scientific methods, processes, and systems to extract knowledge or insights from various data forms and is similar to data mining.

DECISION TREES: A decision tree is a graph that uses a branching method to illustrate every possible outcome of a decision.

DEEP LEARNING (DL): Also known as deep structured learning or hierarchical learning, deep learning is part of a broader family of machine learning methods based on learning data representations, as opposed to task-specific algorithms.

DEEP NEURAL NETWORK (DNN): Deep neural networks are components of larger machine-learning applications involving algorithms for reinforcement learning, classification, and regression.

DIGITAL JOURNEY: A context-aware interaction between an end user and a brand or business whereby the interaction becomes a digital conversation in which technology establishes and builds a powerful experience with deep emotional connections through three key values: simplification, surprise, and anticipation.

DIGITAL NATIVE: A person or a company born in the digital era and defined by their approach to technology that embraces a lean software practice willing to try, fail, and try again with an entrepreneurial start-up. This can also refer to an innovative technology company whose new products redefine and drastically boost user experience and engagement. The term is attributed to educational consultant Marc Prensky, who coined it to refer to children raised in a digital, media-saturated world who require a media-rich learning environment to hold their attention.

ENSEMBLE: An ensemble is an arrangement of several different models with a mechanism to reconcile their responses, which in practice has shown to give better performance and generalization capabilities.

GENERATIVE ADVERSARIAL NETWORK (GAN): Generative adversarial networks are a class of artificial intelligence algorithms used in supervised machine learning, implemented by a system of two neural networks competing with each other in a zero-sum game framework.

GRAPHIC PROCESSING UNITS (GPU): A programmable logic chip (processor) specialized for display functions, rendering images, animations, and video for a computer screen.

IBM WATSON: Watson was originally a question-answering computer system capable of answering questions posed in natural language, developed in IBM's DeepQA project by a research team led by principal investigator David Ferrucci. Today the term *Watson* generally refers to IBM's brand of cognitive services.

MACHINE LEARNING (ML): Machine learning is a field of computer science that gives computers the ability to learn without being explicitly programmed.

NAIVE BAYES: In machine learning, naive Bayes classifiers are a family of simple probabilistic classifiers based on applying Bayes's theorem with strong (naive) independence assumptions between the features.

NATURAL LANGUAGE UNDERSTANDING (NLU): In the complicated endeavor of making computers understand human language and communication, NLU aims to extract context, intention, and desired action.

NEURAL NETWORKS: Artificial neural networks (ANNs) or connectionist systems are computing systems inspired by the biological neural networks that constitute animal brains. Such systems learn (progressively improve performance on) tasks by considering examples, generally without task-specific programming.

PERSONALITY INSIGHTS: IBM's Personality Insights service uses linguistic analytics to infer the personality traits ("Big Five"), intrinsic needs, and values of individuals from communications that the user makes available via mediums such as email, text messages, tweets, and forum posts to understand your customers' habits and preferences on an individual level, and at scale.

PROCESS OPTIMIZATION: The discipline of adjusting a process so as to optimize some specified set of parameters without violating some constraint. The most common goals are minimizing cost and maximizing throughput and/or efficiency. This is one of the major quantitative tools in industrial decision-making.

RECOMMENDER SYSTEM: A subclass of information filtering system that seeks to predict the "rating" or "preference" that a user would give to an item.

RECURRENT NEURAL NETWORK (RNN): A class of artificial neural network where connections between units form a directed cycle. This allows it to exhibit dynamic temporal behavior.

REGRESSION: This refers to a mathematical or statistical technique used to estimate the relationships among variables.

REGRESSION TREE: A data-analysis method that recursively partitions data into sets, each of which are simply modeled using regression methods.

REINFORCEMENT LEARNING: Inspired by behaviorist psychology, this area of machine learning allows machines and software agents to automatically determine the ideal behavior within a specific context.

REVENUE OPTIMIZATION: Revenue optimization is the strategic management of pricing, inventory, demand and distribution channels to maximize revenue growth over the long term. It uses demand modeling, demand forecasting, pricing optimization, consumer-behavior predictions and other activities to ensure the right products are sold to the right customers at the right time and for the right price.

SUPERVISED LEARNING: The majority of practical machine learning uses supervised learning. Supervised learning involves the process of an algorithm learning from the training dataset, which has "labels" or a "ground truth," meaning there is an explicit marking of what constitutes a correct answer.

SUPPORT VECTOR MACHINES: In machine learning, support vector machines are supervised learning models with associated learning algorithms that analyze data used for classification and regression analysis.

TENSORFLOW: This is an open-source software library for dataflow programming across a range of tasks. It is a symbolic math library and also used for machine learning applications such as neural networks.

TENSOR PROCESSING UNITS (TPU): Developed by Google, this refers to an AI accelerator application-specific integrated circuit (ASIC) designed specifically for neural network machine learning.

TIME SERIES MODELS: These are methods for analyzing time series data in order to extract meaningful statistics and other characteristics of the data. Time series forecasting is the use of a model to predict future values based on previously observed values.

UNSUPERVISED LEARNING: This is a type of machine learning algorithm used to draw inferences from "unlabeled" data and used to find the structure and relationships between different inputs. The most common unsupervised learning method is cluster analysis, used to find hidden patterns or grouping in data.

VISUAL RECOGNITION: A service that uses deep learning algorithms to analyze images for scenes, objects, faces, and other content (used in the IBM Watson Visual Recognition). The response includes keywords that provide information about the content.

REFERENCES

Cognitive Computing Consortium.
cognitivecomputingconsortium.com.

Goodfellow, Ian, Yoshua Bengio, and Aaron Courville. *Deep Learning*. Cambridge, MA: MIT Press, 2016.

Google Cloud Platform. *Cloud AI*. cloud.google.com/
products/machine-learning.

Hinton, Geoffrey E., and Ruslan R. Salakhutdinov.
"Reducing the Dimensionality of Data with Neural
Networks." *Science* 313(5786) (July 28, 2006): 504–507.
www.cs.toronto.edu/~hinton/science.pdf.

Horowitz, Andreessen. *AI Playbook*. aiplaybook.a16z.com.

Hutchins, John. "The first public demonstration of machine
translation: the Georgetown-IBM system, 7th January
1954." www.hutchinsweb.me.uk/GU-IBM-2005.pdf.

IBM. *701 Translator*. Press release, January 1954. www-03.
ibm.com/ibm/history/exhibits/701/701_translator.html.

———. *Watson*. www.ibm.com/watson.

"Language and Machines: Computers in Translation and
Linguistics." Automatic Language Processing Advisory
Committee, Division of Behavioral Sciences. National
Academy of Sciences, National Research Council,

Publication 1416 (1966). www.mt-archive.info/
ALPAC-1966.pdf.

Le, Quoc V. "Building high-level features using large scale
unsupervised learning." *IEEE Xplore Digital Library*. May
2013. ieeexplore.ieee.org/document/6639343.

LeCun, Yann, Yoshua Bengio, and Geoffrey Hinton. "Deep
Learning." *Nature* 521(7553) (May 28, 2015): 436–444.
www.nature.com/articles/nature14539.

Martín, Jesús. "Design Framework for Chatbots." *Chatbots
Magazine*. February 23, 2017. chatbotsmagazine.com/
design-framework-for-chatbots-aa27060c4ea3.

Matiisen, Tambet. "Demystifying Deep Reinforcement
Learning." *Intel AI*. December 22, 2015.
www.intelnervana.com/demystifying-deep-
reinforcement-learning/.

Microsoft. *Bot Framework*. dev.botframework.com.

———. *Cognitive Toolkit*. www.microsoft.com/en-us/
cognitive-toolkit.

Microsoft Azure. *Cognitive Services*. azure.microsoft.com/en-
us/services/cognitive-services.

Mnih, Volodymyr, Koray Kavukcuoglu, David Silver, Alex
Graves, Ioannis Antonoglou, Daan Wierstra, and Martin
Riedmiller. *Playing Atari with Deep Reinforcement
Learning*. DeepMind Technologies. December 13, 2013.
arxiv.org/pdf/1312.5602.pdf.

Mnih, Volodymyr, Koray Kavukcuoglu, David Silver, Andrei
A. Rusu, Joel Veness, Marc G. Bellemare, Alex Graves,
Martin Riedmiller, Andreas K Fidjeland, Georg Ostrovski,

et al. "Human-level control through deep reinforcement learning." *Nature* 518(7540) (February 26, 2015): 529–533. www.nature.com/articles/nature14236?page=4.

Murphy, Juan José López. "Survival of the Fittest: The AI Gold Rush." *DZone.* June 1, 2017. dzone.com/articles/survival-of-the-fittest-the-ai-gold-rush.

Ng, Andrew. "AI Is the New Electricity." *Wall Street Journal* video. June 9, 2017. on.wsj.com/2tc3gLU.

———. "Deep Learning." Coursera. www.deeplearning.ai.

Nielsen, Michael A. *Neural Networks and Deep Learning.* Determination Press (2015). neuralnetworksanddeeplearning.com.

PyTorch. *Tensors and Dynamic neural networks in Python with strong GPU acceleration.* pytorch.org.

Raval, Siraj, Andrew Trask, Ian Goodfellow. "Deep Learning." Nanodegree Foundation Program. www.udacity.com/course/deep-learning-nanodegree-foundation--nd101.

Rogati, Monica. "The AI Hierarchy of Needs." *Hackernoon.* August 1, 2017. hackernoon.com/the-ai-hierarchy-of-needs-18f111fcc007.

Rosenblatt, Frank. *The Perceptron: A Perceiving and Recognizing Automaton (Project Para).* Cornell Aeronautical Laboratory, January 1957. blogs.umass.edu/brain-wars/files/2016/03/rosenblatt-1957.pdf.

Russell, Stuart, Peter Norvig. *Artificial Intelligence: A Modern Approach,* 3rd ed. Prentice Hall Series in Artificial Intelligence. 2003. aima.cs.berkeley.edu.

Schmidhuber, Jürgen. "Deep Learning in Neural Networks: An Overview." *Neural Networks* 61 (January 2015): 85–117. arxiv.org/abs/1404.7828.

TensorFlow. *An open-source software library for Machine Intelligence.* www.tensorflow.org.

Van Veen, Fjodor. "The Neural Network Zoo." *The Asimov Institute.* September 14, 2016. www.asimovinstitute.org/neural-network-zoo.

"World Economic Forum White Paper: Digital Transformation of Industries: Accenture. Digital Enterprise." *World Economic Forum.* January 2016. reports.weforum.org/digital-transformation/wp-content/blogs.dir/94/mp/files/pages/files/digital-enterprise-narrative-final-january-2016.pdf.

Weizenbaum, Joseph. *Eliza: A Computer Program for the Study of Natural Language Communication Between Man and Machine.* Communications of the ACM 9(1) (1966): 36–45. dl.acm.org/citation.cfm?id=365168.

ACKNOWLEDGMENTS

E MBRACING THE POWER OF AI has been our second company-wide journey to create a book—in this case, to share the exciting developments and opportunities of AI technologies. We are grateful for the expertise and input provided by our broad spectrum of Globers and the engineers, technologists, and colleagues we partner with. We hope it will resonate with you and help illuminate a path for the ways in which AI can be unleashed and harnessed for your business or industry. This book represents Globant's vision in this new era of AI and explores how it synchronizes with our work with partners and customers. It was an extremely rewarding process and we hope that every reader taps into the enthusiasm and inspiration we experienced in writing it.

Our special thanks to Javier Minhondo, Juan José López Murphy, Haldo Spontón, Martin Migoya, and Guibert Englebienne in helping drive the valuable contents of this book. We also want to recognize Carolina Dolan and Wanda Weigert for helping make this idea come true. Lastly, our recognition goes to Roundtree Press for their skilled staff of editorial and graphic designers who worked diligently alongside us to polish and realize a book that we're proud to share with all of our customers, partners, and colleagues.

Special thanks to all the Globers who participated with ideas and actual implementations of AI. They provided the kinds of insights and perspectives that we can now showcase to help others gain inspiration to put AI to work in their respective businesses.

Globant (NYSE:GLOB) is a digitally native technology services company. We are passionate about building the new way of being digital. We want to help our clients emotionally connect with consumers and employees, leveraging the power of artificial intelligence for business optimization. We are the place where engineering, design, and innovation meet scale. For more information visit www.globant.com.

AUTHORS

JAVIER MINHONDO

Javier is a devoted and passionate software engineer with years of experience. As the vice president of technology of the Artificial Intelligence Studio at Globant, he engages with companies to enhance digital journeys by leveraging cognitive and emotional aspects with the ever-increasing capacity of machines to learn and understand complex patterns. He utilizes state-of-the-art techniques, including deep learning, neural networks, or traditional machine learning approaches, coupled with hacking and engineering abilities.

JUAN JOSÉ LÓPEZ MURPHY

Juan's primary area of interest is working on the intersection of innovation, strategy, technology, and data. He is passionate about data, whether from a data science, data engineering, or BI data visualization mind-set, always looking for the ways in which technology enables and is the driver of business model innovation—true disruption is the result of both.

HALDO SPONTÓN

Haldo is an eager technology and math lover, with vast experience as a teacher and researcher in signal processing and machine learning. He's part of the leadership team of our Artificial Intelligence Studio at Globant. He's focused on the usage of AI algorithms in end-to-end applications, combining user experience, business needs, and technology innovation.

MARTÍN MIGOYA

In 2003, Martín, with only a small start-up capital, co-founded Globant with three friends. Fifteen years after its launch, Martín drove the company as CEO from a small start-up to a publicly listed organization with more than 6,700+ professionals, pushing the edge of innovative digital journeys in offices across the globe. Martín, whose passion is to inspire future entrepreneurs, frequently gives lectures to foster the entrepreneurship gene, and has won numerous prestigious industry awards, including the E&Y Entrepreneur of the Year award.

GUIBERT ENGLEBIENNE

Guibert has had a lifelong passion for cutting-edge technology and exploring how it fits into business and culture. He is one of Globant's cofounders and now serves as CTO leading the execution of thousands of consumer-facing technology projects. He is a frequent speaker and thinker on how to drive a culture of innovation at scale in organizations. Guibert is widely recognized as one of the industry's most influential leaders.

Hardcover ISBN: 978-1-944903-52-7
E-book ISBN: 978-1-944903-64-0

Managing Editor: *Lee Bruno*
Editor: *Jan Hughes*
Proofreader: *Mason Harper*
Book and jacket design: *Iain R. Morris*

Printed in the United States of America
10 9 8 7 6 5 4 3 2 1

Library of Congress Cataloging-in-Publication Data available.

 Roundtree Press

149 Kentucky Street, Suite 7
Petaluma, CA 94952

www.roundtreepress.com